SILHOUETTES OF PEKING

BY
D. DE MARTEL
& L. DE HOYER
TRANSLATED BY
D. DE WARZEE

EARNSHAW BOOKS

Silhouettes Of Peking

ISBN-13: 978-988-19090-4-6

© 2010 Earnshaw Books

Originally published by China Booksellers Ltd. Peking 1926

This book has been reset in 10pt Book Antiqua. Spellings and punctuations are left as in the original edition.

HISTORY / Asia / China

EB038

All rights reserved. No part of this book may be reproduced in material form, by any means, whether graphic, electronic, mechanical or other, including photocopying or information storage, in whole or in part. May not be used to prepare other publications without written permission from the publisher except in the case of brief quotations embodied in critical articles or reviews. For information contact info@earnshawbooks.com

Published by Earnshaw Books Ltd. (Hong Kong)

FOREWORD

THE AUTHORS

IN 1926 the expatriate community in China was bracing itself for an uncertain future. The previous year British policemen in Shanghai had shot several students protesting against imperialism. Commerce was still suffering from the subsequent general strike. Now China was in a state of civil war. From Canton, the 'Northern Expedition', an army consisting of Nationalists and Communists, was advancing towards Wuhan, easily smashing the warlord forces ranged against them. Nobody was clear as to what the Nationalist leader, General Chiang Kai-shek, wanted, but they feared the worst. With his Russian advisers, Galen and Borodin, he was thought to be as Red as his paymaster Stalin. Western interests seemed threatened. The International Concession in Shanghai was taking all precautions. Its boulevards began to sprout barbed wire and sandbags as British troops patrolled the streets.

It was therefore a welcome diversion in this charged up atmosphere when the small Peking publishing house, China Booksellers, produced a slim novel, rumored to be wickedly salacious and gorgeously illustrated by the popular Shanghai artist and cartoonist, Sapajou. The biggest surprise, however, was that one of the authors of this scandalous sensation was the Minister of the French Legation in Peking, the seasoned diplomat, Le Comte Damien de Martel. The foreign community forgot their troubles and scattered off to the beach resorts in Tsingtao and Peitaiho, copies of *Silhouettes of Peking* in their hand luggage.

What they read was sheer escapism. The delicious *roman* took them away from the louring tensions of the revolutionary 1920s, back a decade to the early days of the Chinese Republic. In their minds that had been a golden age, the China many dreamed of when they took the steamer from Europe. Nobody then was threatened by warlords or Bolsheviks. An amenable military strongman, Yuan Shikai, listened respectfully to the top-hatted representatives of the Powers, who in their leisure moments lived a luxurious existence, dining, racing and picnicking among the picturesque ruins of a romantic Imperial China.

The novel was also exquisitely decadent, and not just a little *risqué* (very French, of course). Tongues must have been wagging, wondering quite who the very respectable French Minister was basing his characters upon (everybody would have known he was Chargé d'Affaires in Peking in 1916, the period in which the story was set).

There was also something of a mystery. Who was the co-author, *L. de Hoyer*? The older scions in the banking community, relishing their inside knowledge, would have gauged the right moment at the dinner table to reveal his identity: Léon Viktorovich de Hoyer, yes, that's right, Baron de Hoyer – the notorious Russian financier, Peking head of the Banque Russo-Chinoise, whose devious reputation had earned him the sobriquet, "Intrigue personified as a man."[1] Eight years earlier, his public feud with Damien de Martel had rocked the diplomatic and business community in Peking, and only ended when the Count, using the influence of the French Government, had secured de Hoyer's dismissal from China. They were, and probably still were, the bitterest of enemies.

"So how was it they collaborated on a novel?" the puzzled audience would have asked.

"Ah, that is the mystery, and the tragedy," the banker would have sighed. "Did you not know? They were once the greatest of friends."

Looking through the scanty records today, much remains hypothetical, but some facts are clear. When the Comte de Martel took up his posting in Peking in 1913, de Hoyer would have been high on his list of important contacts. And we can assume there was immediate rapport. Partly it was a matter of class. Both men were aristocrats (de Hoyer of Baltic nobility and de Martel of ancient knightly lineage) and they were also senior civil servants used to moving in the highest circles. De Martel's diplomatic career had taken him to Petrograd before coming to Peking. In all probability he would already have heard of de Hoyer who had once worked in the Russian Finance Ministry. He would certainly have come across the Banque Russo-Asiatique (the BRA, Russia's largest bank and the parent of the Banque Russo-Chinoise). The BRA was in fact a vital French interest, for although it was an arm of the Russian Government, actually a third of its capital investment came

---

1. 'From Revolution to Dissolution: The Quai d'Orsay, the Banque Russo-Asiatique and the Chinese Eastern Railway – 1917-1926', by Michael Carley, *International History Review*, Vol. 12, No. 4 (Nov 1990).

from France. In China its role was political as much as it was commercial: the subsidiary run by de Hoyer was the sole stockholder of the Russian-controlled China Eastern Railway and one of the three Custodian banks for customs revenues.[2] It was a vehicle for Russian imperial penetration, and also for that of France, a commercial fig leaf for both countries' colonial ambitions. So it was not surprising that in the small Peking community, the two men saw a lot of each other: the French diplomat and the man who handled France's investments were drawn together as much for professional reasons as social.

More importantly, they shared a similar temperament and interests outside their work. They were intellectuals, fascinated by China's history and politics, and also, particularly in de Hoyer's case, the philosophy of the East.[3] Above all they were men of the world, in their mid-thirties, attracted by material wealth and beautiful women, practised in the fashionable dalliances and intrigues of their class. And at some point, probably in 1916 or 1917, they decided to collaborate to write *Silhouettes of Peking*. They wrote in French, of course, the first language of Frenchmen, diplomats and Russian aristocrats, as well as the perfect medium for *fin de siècle* sensuality and exoticism.

Perhaps they intended to publish, perhaps only to circulate the manuscript among their friends. Whatever their intentions, the Bolshevik Revolution in Russia changed both their lives and delayed publication for a decade. It also destroyed their friendship.

---

2. Foreigners since the nineteenth century had controlled the collection of Imperial Customs dues and tax, and these sums of money were channeled to the Chinese Government through foreign banks.

3. In later life he was to write a book called *Meditations on Plato and Buddha*.

When the Bolsheviks confiscated all the Tsarist banks in early 1918, the BRA was left only with its assets abroad, and most of these were in China. Bureaucrats in the Quai d'Orsay in Paris suddenly saw an opportunity. Following the confiscations inside Russia, most of the capital left to the BRA was French – in China this amounted to three quarters of the capital stock. For the more aggressively imperialist among them – and de Martel was one of these – it seemed only right that since the bulk of the money was theirs they should control the assets, including the China Eastern Railway. Russians of the old regime, however, like de Hoyer, believed that what had been kept out of the hands of the Bolsheviks should remain in theirs. De Hoyer's business ethics, and those of his boss in the BRA, the plutocrat Putilov (by now in exile in Shanghai), may have been questionable (it was rumored that they both had made fortunes out of war speculation before the revolution), but for all his flaws de Hoyer seems to have been moved by patriotism. It took the form of negotiating behind de Martel's back with the Chinese Government to establish a new ownership of the Railway with a board consisting entirely of Russians, cutting out the French. For good measure, he also negotiated with the Japanese and the Americans. De Martel, who felt betrayed by his old friend, used his Government influence to have de Hoyer sacked. Putilov accepted the loss of his right-hand man because the codicil was that the French Government would compromise on a wholly Russian board. In other words, though de Martel had his revenge on de Hoyer, France lost the railway. Martel had been pursuing "personal policies," was Putilov's cynical quip.[4]

---

4. Carley, 'From Revolution to Dissolution'.

The friends-turned-enemies left Peking at about the same time – de Hoyer to Harbin where he continued to intrigue, de Martel to promotion and a glittering foreign office career. 1919 found him in the Caucasus as Allied High Commissioner in Siberia during the Civil War (he was later to be demonised in the Bolshevik ballet 'The Siege of Perekop') and the following year he became Minister in Riga, capital of Latvia. He arrived back in Peking as Minister in 1924, ironically to preside over the final collapse of the BRA (in the end the Peking Government did what was sensible, preferring to deal no longer with the White Russians, handing over the China Eastern Railway to the Bolsheviks despite the manoeuvrings of de Hoyer, who remained a thorn in France's side until the very end).

The question only remained: why, in 1926, did de Martel go ahead with the publication of a book in which his name was associated with that of his enemy?[5] It seems on the face of it strange that there could have been reconciliation after such a bitter feud. On the other hand, perhaps all the savage feelings engendered by the long wars and controversies that followed the Revolution had burned themselves out among those involved, leaving only remorse and regret? Perhaps de Martel had heard that de Hoyer, like many White Russians, had fallen on hard times and thought that income from a youthful *oeuvre* might help

---

5. Incidentally the novel, written first in French, was now being published, for commercial reasons, in English. Things had changed in 10 years and now English was the lingua franca, at least on the China Coast. But the aristocratic stamp on the work remained. It was a member of the Belgian nobility, Dorothy de Warzee, Baroness d'Hermaille, wife of the Counsellor in the Belgian Ministry in Peking, Le Maire de Warzee, Baron d'Hermaille, who was invited to do the translation. She had some experience, having translated the travel guide *Peeps from Persia* in 1915 during a previous posting.

him. One likes to think that it was generosity rather than vanity that impelled de Martel to go to print. The truth is we don't know. Nor do we know whether it was de Hoyer's initiative or that of de Martel that caused the book to be published. The fact that the illustrator was a Russian artist, Georgi Avksentievich Sapojnikoff, better known as Sapajou, who was famous between the Wars as the political cartoonist on Shanghai's *North-China Daily News* and *North-China Herald*,[6] may have been the result of a connection with his fellow Russian, de Hoyer. Alternatively, Sapajou may have been an acquaintance of de Martel's (senior diplomats then as now cultivated celebrities and opinion makers in the societies in which they were posted). Or the publisher may have commissioned him. Again we don't know.

We do have quite a bit of information about the later professional life of Damien de Martel, because he was much mentioned in newspapers. We see him taking a French gunboat from Tsingtao to Hankow in 1928 where he praised the Nationalist Revolution and offered France's support to Chiang Kai-shek (the civil war hadn't ended but everybody could see which way the wind was blowing). In 1930 (just before leaving China to become Ambassador in Japan) he delivered a strong 'Note' to the Chinese Government stating that France would oppose the unilateral abrogation of 'Extrality'[7] (this time he apparently failed to see which way the wind was blowing). He ended his career as High

---

6. Sapajou's cartoons can now be enjoyed again in his *Collected Works*, republished by Earnshaw Books.

7. Privileges granted to foreigners under the 'Unequal Treaties' of the nineteenth century, allowing them to run their own trading concessions and be immune to Chinese law.

Commissioner of French Mandated Syria. He was respected for his strong stance against terrorists but the problems he faced were intractable and he left in 1939 amid political chaos, dying of a heart attack in Paris a few months later.

Léon de Hoyer also died in Paris in 1939. He had spent his last few years writing, one suspects in poverty, a bitter exile since the Japanese had exerted control over Harbin in 1931. He spent much of his time thinking of his lost Tsarist homeland and wondering where things first went wrong. He put his thoughts into a 500-page novel, called *Les Précurseurs*, about nihilists in Russia in the 1860s, but he did not live to see it published. It did not remain in print long.

Ironically, despite their turbulent lives and the momentous political events in which they were involved, all that remains to remember either of these men is the 200-page *divertissement* they wrote together, in their converted Chinese courtyard houses decorated with Turkish divans and Chinese curios, or at a summer bungalow in Shanhaikuan or Peitaiho, during their happy years working together in Peking.

THE NOVEL

Silhouettes of Peking is one of a remarkable number of excellent novels written in the early years of the twentieth century by expatriates living in Peking. Authors were aesthetes like Sir Harold Acton,[8] diplomats like Daniele Varè,[9] travelers like W. Somerset Maugham,[10] and 'spouses' like

---

8. *Peonies and Ponies.*
9. *The Maker of Heavenly Trousers, The Gate of Happy Sparrows, The Temple of Costly Experience.*
10. *On A Chinese Screen.*

Anne Bridge.[11] It is from these novels, as well as the memoirs of Sir Reginald Johnston,[12] John Blofeld[13] and George Kates,[14] and guidebooks like Nagel and Juliet Bredon's *Peking*, that we draw our very vivid portrait of the rarefied life these privileged foreigners experienced. If there is one word that always is repeated it is "magic". *Silhouettes of Peking* takes an honorable place in the pantheon but stands out for one particular reason. While most of these books were written for an English-speaking readership, *Silhouettes* was originally written in French, and its sensibility is Gallic, from its first page on.

Early in *Silhouettes* a diplomat, Baron de Beaurelois, calls on the hero (or perhaps more appropriately anti-hero), the intellectual Maugrais, in his exquisitely decorated Peking apartment. Maugrais greets him in a 'negligée' (the characters in this *roman* are forever getting into and out of native dress for their opium smoking or *amours*, or merely to indulge their *ennui*). The Baron, it transpires, has been sent by his wife, the beautiful Blanche, to lure Maugrais to dinner. Maugrais knows (although the cuckold husband apparently doesn't) that she will attempt to seduce him, but he suspects that another siren will be there – Madame de Beaurelois's competitor, the dazzling Mrs Brixton, wife of an American diplomat, who also wants Maugrais as a trophy. Of the two, she is the deadlier, because she is alluring – diabolically so – and Maugrais is determined not to fall into either of their traps...

Such is the decadent picture the two authors draw of expatriate life in China's capital in the years after the 1911 revolution, a society of glittering birds of passage on three- or four-year postings in which they may indulge

---

11. *Peking Picnic, The Ginger Griffin.*
12. *Twilight in the Forbidden City.*
13. *City of Lingering Splendour.*
14. *The Years That Were Fat.*

themselves in all the pleasures that a grand and mysterious civilization in decline has to offer. The 'smart set' as they call themselves, are forever vying with each other to throw the grandest banquet or to collect the rarest antique; riding their ponies to ruined palaces for soirées or picnics; or commandeering ancient temples at the seaside resort of Shanhaikuan to indulge their adulterous affairs.

Maugrais describes his circle sardonically:

> Peking is a city of officials, slightly formal and perhaps a trifle snobbish, but anyway clean-minded and agreeable to frequent. It is a casual and temporary agglomeration of people who have seen the world, have stayed in Paris and London; passed through Florence and Athens, played with politics in Petrograd or with finance in America; people who have crossed all the seas, made collections in the East and made love in Venice…but it is above everything else, a city that has given birth to a special type of human being…the Peking silhouette.

The silhouette image of the title touches what is perhaps the main theme of the novel. Despite their brilliance, foreigners are doomed only to touch the surface of a society which they can but imperfectly understand. Ultimately their exquisite and hedonistic life is artificial and unsatisfying.

There are very few actual Chinese in these pages except the ubiquitous 'boys' and *mafoos* who serve the smart set, and the peasants they encounter on the roads on their outings. The Chinese they do socialize with are senior members of the government who have undergone various degrees of westernization. Yet 'China' – or rather the Orientalized and Romantic version of it they choose to conjure – is in fact the most insidious temptress of them all, and perhaps the central character in this story.

SILHOUETTES OF PEKING

As the novel progresses we see Maugrais and some of the other foreigners struggling with the enigma of being a cosmopolitan living in an ancient and alien culture, which is at the same time a well of both dark depravity and spiritual wisdom. And there is a choice to be made between innocence and evil. The American, Mrs Brixton, is a predator but her power and sensuality seem to draw their force from the irresistible melancholy in the beauty around them. Picnicking in the ruins of an imperial palace, the Wan Hai Lo, the party is told of the doomed and tragic love affair between the Emperor Qian Long and the Uighur princess, Xiang Fei (the Fragrant Concubine). It is a tale that drips with the gloomy romance of Galland's *Arabian Nights*. It is in this corruptive atmosphere that Mrs Brixton snares her victim, igniting a love that "flames like Lucifer himself come straight from Hell."

> Millions of stars twinkled in the dark and solemn sky, speaking to each other through the infinite space in a mute luminous language of flashes of light. They called up the memory of ages buried in the unfathomable mystery of the past and announced the coming of centuries of unrelenting time…And all appeal from Here Below was unanswered. No sound reached the bottomless pit where for countless years human pain and misery had been swallowed up, where oceans of blood and floods of tears will be shed until the end of time…Lying on the grass his eyes fixed on the dark firmament, Maugrais was now quite still and the immensity of his love soared in communion with the infinite.

It is of course inevitable that Maugrais comes to repent what he sees later as his fall, and perhaps also inevitable that the book ends on a quest for something spiritual. After all that's what all the Buddhas and Guanyins that the smart set collect actually represent – and the 1910s, post Theosophy, Gurdjieff and Diaghelev, were indeed a time when 'the ancient wisdom of the East' was getting a fashionable vogue.

But the book is saved from pretentiousness, and its occasional passages of purple prose do not ultimately offend, because one suspects a certain degree of outrageousness was built into the authors' intentions from the start.

For there is a deliberate element of self-mockery about *Silhouettes of Peking*. We know only a little about the authors but what we do shows them to have been of exactly the class and profession of the characters in their novel. One suspects that Le Comte de Martel and the Baron de Hoyer were indulging themselves in a grand *jeu d'ésprit*, an entertainment for their friends in the diplomatic corps whom they had known in Peking in the days before and during the First World War, and who were almost certainly intended to recognize themselves in the fictional representations, partly celebrating, partly satirizing the fabulous life they had lived.

What the two authors achieved was an exquisite *bon bon*, or a finely packaged jewel. It was intended to be luxurious and slightly wicked, as is good chocolate. Can one not see a Lautrec-type poster of this scene in an opium den?

> The Baroness floating in a sea of love and kindness, her dress open, her beautiful bosom bare, said to the Count, 'No, my friend, I am afraid of growing old, afraid of the old age of ugliness and death. I want to live, to love, to bestow myself endlessly, to be born again, to live again, to bestow myself on the whole world.'

And the ribbon that ties this glorious chocolate box, as readers will see in this newly published edition, are the

45 glorious illustrations by the incomparable and much-loved Sapajou. The full range of his capabilities can be seen in the drawings here, perfectly capturing the changing moods of this book from the hilarious (the drawing of the ridiculous Chatours in the theater box with Chinese actors in his attempts to go native), to the picturesque (scenes of the outskirts of Peking that exactly match the fine prose descriptions) to the whimsical (cartoons of opium pipes, policemen, geishas and gods).

The book was designed as a treasure, a *memento* for a future generation of a romantic past – and therefore there is a strain of melancholy throughout (but that too is self-indulgent, like a recording of Stravinsky played on a gramophone on a balmy summer evening).

The novel echoes several peculiarly French genres:

- The comedy of manners and corruption – the sexual plotting of the Baroness Beaurelois and Mrs Brixton are a pale imitation of *Les Liaisons Dangereuses*;
- The sensual allure of native cultures – one thinks of Gauguin, Marguerite Duras and J M G de Clézio at the high end and *Emmanuelle* at the bottom; this book comes somewhere in between;
- The fabulous romances with Oriental themes, favored by La Fontaine and Galland;
- The *fin de siècle* melodramas in high-blown classical language like 'Salome'.

Traces of all of these styles can be found in its pages. It perhaps took a later, greater writer, the Italian Daniele Varè, who had also been a diplomat in Peking in the 1910s, to make a truly original literary masterpiece out of similar themes: colorful, curious China; the temptations into decadence; the call of the spirit, a.k.a. wisdom of the Orient; the aesthetes; the curio collectors; the impeccable taste of a European who has got to know a different culture, etc.

But to say that *Silhouettes* is 'light' or 'ephemeral' is no criticism of de Martel and de Hoyer who, after all, were originally only engaged in a private amusement for their own set of friends.

What they have left behind, for a new generation of expatriates in China, is a confectionery of the past, not as it really was but as they, and perhaps we, would (in our secret heart of hearts) have liked it to have been.

Adam Williams
Peking
May 2010

SILHOUETTES OF PEKING
CHAPTER I

JEAN Maugrais, pulling towards him the last sofa cushion that still shewed some reluctance to accommodate itself to the soft outline of his body, felt so unutterably comfortable that he threw up his eyes with a look of gratitude towards the mauve storks on the ceiling.

Pale blue stripes, like small snakes ran all over his pink silk pyjamas. His dainty slippers lay unheeded on the arabesques of the carpet, and as the smoke from his cigarette formed delicate halos round his head, his eyes rested tenderly on the gilding of the lacquer furniture, on the delightfully faded yellow of the old silks and on the insolently vivid colourings of his old Chinese porcelain. To him it was all voluptuousness. At moments during this warm and religious Sunday morning, he seemed to hear hymns of peace and happiness murmuring in his ear.

Breaking the silence that reigned in the room he spoke aloud to himself:

"The anticipation of a whole day of solitude makes me feel good. I cannot imagine embittered men existing, on whom life weighs as heavily as a leaden cross; or scatter-brains who throw themselves into passions and hurl themselves into catastrophes like moths into the flame of a candle; or that there are women like Mrs. Brixton, Mme. de Beaurelois and many others who seek complicated adventures outside their own homes and their placid lives.

"A little philosophy will make for much happiness. What is that particular thing we seek for so clumsily at times? Nothing at all in reality, simply tranquillity, health, careless generosity and contagious examples. Is it really possible that those who have suffered most, if they could see me now and could read my soul, would be unable to forget their own unhappiness, and could share, without depriving me, my happiness. . . . . I have never felt my heart so light, so full of kindness and gentle love towards every one as I do to-day. . . . ."

But suddenly his eyes fell on a blue vase placed on a small Cantonese wood table. He was conscious of a change coming over him; his boy persisted in turning towards the wall the best side of the jar — the four bonzes parading in a fancy landscape — the unadorned side of the piece of porcelain being exposed. "The lack of imagination and artistic sense is really disgusting, especially in direct descendants of the great potters of the Ming dynasty, the magnificent century of Kang Hsi." And while these thoughts were passing through his mind, he grew angrier with his boy for the slight interest he took in works of art and also for having broken his charming dream of peace and quiet. He was even about to ring to tell the boy, probably in very unamiable terms, what he thought of him when the bell sounded. Maugrais hesitated a second, contemplating with a slight shudder the electric button, then, suddenly understanding that the maker of this noise could only be a visitor, he sought uneasily for some excuse forbidding his entrance. A door squeaked and a slender Chinese, his pigtail swinging back and fro, went towards the front door. Maugrais had just time to make him two signs as he passed, one meaning "in the drawing room opposite" the other "close the door." He tried to recognise the voice speaking in the hall, but was unsuccessful. So he waited with the patience of a fatalist for enlightenment about the intruder. The boy came back with a card. Maugrais read the name, Baron Louis de Beaurelois.

"At least he is not dangerous," said Jean, but all the same he was annoyed at being disturbed.

"He is a good sort, frank and candid. . . . . and perhaps not so stupid as he is supposed to be. . ." He slipped his feet into his slippers, threw his cigarette away and adopting a surprised and happy air, went to meet the enemy.

"My dear Beaurelois, how nice of you to come and see me; here, let's have a cocktail," and he signed to the boy to bring him the necessary ingredients.

"Are you alone," asked Beaurelois discreetly, glancing at the elegant negligée Jean was wearing.

"Forgive me," he said, "I have not been up long and I did not feel in the least inclined to dress. Had I known you were coming". . . . .

"You would have been wrong to change anything in your appearance," interrupted Beaurelois, "you look very smart like that."

"Come in here, old man, we shall be able to talk better."

He took him into the smoking room where he had meant to pass some delightful hours. After settling his visitor into a comfortable arm chair, he sank into the corner he had just vacated.

"What a varied and magnificient collection of curios," said Beaurelois after a short silence. "Good taste, when it has the luck to be allied with money and curiosity can perform miracles."

As Maugrais busied himself with the cocktails, he thought, "After all, he does not lack judgement and he is friendly and polite."

"I was passing down your street," went on Beaurelois, "and I said to myself, we never see Maugrais any more. If the mountain will not come to me. . . ; and I decided not to abandon you to your solitude until I had got a formal promise that we should soon see you at home."

The cocktails were ready; he took a glass saying as he drank it that it was the best he had ever tasted. Then he continued. "Do you know you have no right to shut yourself up as you do, depriving us of your company. You have certain duties you owe to Society for you are one of the specially chosen. Yes, I am in earnest, you have duties and, by the way, that reminds me of a proposition I should hate to see you refuse. . . ."

"Some new catastrophe threatens me," thought Maugrais. Then addressing himself to his visitor, "If it depends on me, you can be sure. . . . ."

"Well, I will give you my real reason for coming here. My wife was very disappointed when she got your note. She was relying on you for our dinner to-morrow; there will only be a few specially selected and sympathetic people and she is quite upset by your refusal. Make an effort, Maugrais. Do come, you have no valid reason for refusing."

"I am sorrier than you can think, believe me, but. . ."

"Yes, I know, your diet, dry bread and milk at night. You shall have it, I promise you anything you want, though you don't look as if you needed sympathy. You have a splendid colour, and clear eyes and you seem at peace with all the world. We shall all be green with envy to-morrow."

"It is always the way," explained Maugrais who had never before appreciated his robust health as at this moment. "Massage gives me a colour and an air of health so long as I don't move. But as soon as ever I stick my nose out of doors, or I take a few steps towards a rickshaw, I change. My legs wobble, my cheeks grow pallid and I turn giddy. I have been like that for some time, so the doctor has given me strict orders to go to bed at nine regularly for several weeks. Later on I promise you I shall be your most frequent visitor."

"But now I come to think about it," said Beaurelois trying to joke, "you are going to have a great responsibility; for without you we shall be thirteen."

"Touch wood," said Maugrais.

"We thought Brixton would be back by to-morrow but he does not return for another week. Mrs. Brixton is coming alone."

"She is one of your guests to-morrow?"

"Yes, of course. You ask as if that would influence you. I should not be in the least annoyed, however, if we owed your consent to such a powerful ally."

"My dear Beaurelois," said Maugrais seriously, "you are quite wrong, all of you. I know Peking gossips. You will come across 20 people who would swear on the heads of their best friends that they possess absolute proof of our feelings towards each other. It is so amusing to spread a scandal when it is more or less harmless and to embellish it. Can you imagine teas, dinners, picnics where this inexhaustible mine was lacking? Whatever should we talk about? But, one evening, at Mrs. Brixton's—I think by the way you were there,—we seemed to have talked ourselves dry. In spite of bridge and dancing, the air was full of blue devils, the conversation dragged. I must confess I was frankly bored. During dinner I was separated from our hostess by the melancholic and serious old Frissonges but she addressed herself to me more than usual. I think she mingled some subtle innuendoes in her conversation. She seemed to attack me boldly though defending herself cleverly. . . . ." He was silent for a minute, lost in thought.

"She has that very rare gift of being able at times to put so much meaning into a single glance that it takes but a second more to lose one's mental and physical balance. It's a very disagreeable sensation and rather a terrifying one. I sensed it once before in my life in Cairo but then the transmitter was a Spanish woman for whom I had a great admiration and there was no struggle. . . ."

"Really, old man," interrupted Beaurelois interestedly, "is Mrs. Brixton that sort of woman?"

"Always be on your guard," advised Maugrais, laughingly.

"I must tell you everything as there is nothing to confess, and even if there were, forgive me, such a confession to a serious man who does not mix himself up in back door gossip should act as an excellent remedy for my neurasthenia.

"I had sneaked into a small dimly lit room which happened to be empty. I had scarcely settled myself there, when I heard an exclamation of surprise from the doorway, I saw Mrs. Brixton. Her pretty hair was ruffled. She said in a tone impossible to imitate, 'Oh there you are.'

"She came and sat down beside me taking care not to come very close. Suddenly she turned to me and said 'I am bored.' As if in answer to the vague gesture I made, she went on, 'I am sorry I couldn't put you next to me at dinner, but old Frissonges might have been hurt.' And she threw me a glance out of her Gorgon eyes. On a small table by the sofa was a beautiful Grecian head in marble, one of those fragments recently discovered in the Ionian Archipelago, and perhaps to change the subject I said, 'You are lucky to possess such a master-piece of antiquity, it is so much purer and more beautiful than the fantastic morbidities of the East.' 'Yes,' she answered, 'I like that head although it is a little spoilt. When I am nervous or annoyed, bad or sad, I caress the wavy hair; the peaceful coolness of the marble seems to strengthen and console me.' She stretched out her hand and passed her shapely fingers over the head and face; its pristine whiteness was slightly mellowed by age and had become the colour of centuries. Mechanically I put out my hand and touched that gentle face with its ever fixed expression of petrified sadness and desolate innocence. Our hands met on the marble. Thus do the hands of friends meet over the tombstone of the dead. We stayed without moving for some time. I cannot express, for I do not know, what I felt or thought, but when I recovered myself and came out of my dream, for I must have dreamt, Melle de Frissonges and Maxwell were standing behind the sofa looking at us with amused astonishment. I will spare you the rest. You know Maxwell's tongue. All Peking now says—As a matter of fact I don't really know what it does say, but in all probability that I am her lover." Maugrais ceased speaking.

"As for me," said Beaurelois frankly, "I have never heard a word of this, and I don't believe my wife has either."

"You are certainly the only people in Peking, then, for I am neither blind nor deaf and I have noticed how Society cherishes me since that adventure. 'Chance' brings us together all the time. I am under the obligation to redouble my attentions to this woman, to seem mysterious and at the same time familiarly discreet. I have to pretend to seek to meet her eyes while seeming to avoid them . . . and it is really all so different from what my feelings are or from what I should like to do and say . . . ."

"You seem to be complaining," said Beaurelois. "The Youth of the present day is quite incomprehensible; an attractive woman finds you interesting and thinks she can take possession of you. Tired of waiting for you to make the first advances, she pathetically does it herself."

"Oh, no, don't say that, it is not true . . ."

"So you wear a repentant air and weep on my bosom. But tell me, what on earth do you want?"

"Peace," answered Maugrais after a few seconds reflection. "I am now 36; my first love affair dates a long way back. I think I was quite happy then, at least I have looked several times since for the same sweet illusions and probably have not succeeded in finding them. I consider any man over 30 has done all he can in this direction and should begin to try and follow the path of wisdom. Of course I like women and appreciate their society. For any one who flatters himself that he can read even a little into their complicated though frivolous minds, there is still much to learn from them. But if you would avoid suffering, admire them from behind the bars of indifference. Don't stretch out your fingers or you will be bitten; don't offer them your heart for they would burn it for the sole pleasure of playing with the ashes. All that is idiotic, isn't it? I suppose you are astonished that this very acute attack of sentimentality should have led me to become a sort of egoist. But isn't it natural that continuous suffering inspires people, according to their peculiar temperaments, with the firm resolve and the strong desire to suffer no more?"

"You certainly astonish me, Maugrais, for I too have gone through all the usual accidents that happen to bachelors; but I have accepted them calmly. I have not been burnt or become embittered. I finally got married when I was 30 and I am the happiest of husbands."

Maugrais looked at him with a smile as he finished his cigarette. Before the eyes of his mind the beautiful figure of the Baroness flitted, offering herself to love as a flower to the desires of the bee. He asked himself if, after all, it was such a calamity to be betrayed by one's wife.

"So much the better," he said. "You must be an optimist."

"Yes, as much as possible. But your speech does not please me at all. I draw three conclusions from it: (1) You have suffered too, (2) you are afraid of Mrs. Brixton, and (3) we shall be thirteen at table to-morrow."

"Wait a bit," said Maugrais, "I have an idea. The third conclusion is rather troublesome. I see one remedy. Do you know Chatours?"

"Who is Chatours?"

"A young man you ought to know, old man. Besides, he is a friend of mine. I can recommend him unreservedly. Each year, by means that would prove expensive to you or me, he manages to save ten or twelve thousand francs which he immediately spends in Egypt, India or wherever his fancy takes him. This time it is China upon which his choice has fallen. He has been in Peking nearly four months now, in a comfortable Chinese house studying Chinese history, smoking opium in spite of the prohibition, and frequenting only the Chinese with whom he appears already thoroughly at home. He is really very original. He cannot understand living abroad without adopting the customs of the natives and becoming absolutely familiarized with their ways. He thinks European society here only makes the outlook ugly and serves to introduce ideas that are to be deplored."

"Oh, yes, now I remember, I have heard of him . . ."

"Just think, once the 'boy' in a neighbouring *yamen* cut off his pigtail and Chatours gave him to understand that if in a week it had not grown again, he would strangle him for the good of aesthetics. The boy ran away and has never come back. Chatours does nothing like other people. He goes about in a sedan chair and though he often comes to see me for the sake of old times, he has implored me never to try to violate his sanctuary where it is more than probable the most unheard of things occur. I tried sending my boy to have a look round, but he saw no one but a fat old servant, probably an eunuch, who spouted Confucius at him."

"Yes, I have heard people speak of him. He has even managed to get himself a bad reputation in Peking. He was seen, it seems, in a box at the new theatre at Chienmen with some Chinese actors. I think it was he, too, who having tried to rape the daughter of the Chinese ex-Minister to Panama, was very indignant at her resistance and declared that it was in direct contradiction with the characteristic docility and the traditional passiveness of the Eastern woman. I wonder what makes you think such an extraordinary person

would condescend to accept the invitation of a humble Occidental like myself!"

Maugrais got up without answering and left the room. Telephoning to Chatours, he asked him to come round at once and share his lunch.

"You will see," he said when he returned to the smoking room, "the fellow is neither quite wild nor quite civilized.

He is shy like all original people, the sight of a stranger of your colour will put him out of countenance at first. I will begin by asking if he is free to-morrow. Most likely he is; then he will not dare refuse. Besides he likes exaggerating his repugnance for society. He is not really averse to frequenting it. Once the contact is made, he soon discovers the strange undercurrents that influence our sayings and doings. If possible, put him next to Mrs. Brixton. Perhaps that may lead to all sorts of unexpected things."

Ten minutes afterwards, Chatours arrived. His head was completely shaved, but in spite of that, he was rather nice looking, even elegant.

"How handsome you look like that," said Maugrais after the usual introductions.

"It is comfortable," answered Chatours in a tired voice, "and it saves several minutes of absurd labour every day. I have also discovered a temple which, according to some of my Chinese friends, possesses a priest with Tibetan secrets of the greatest importance. I can talk enough Chinese to make myself understood by this sage, and I mean to wring from him some of this knowledge which has been handed down century by century, from the Brahmins to the Lamas, and finally from a Lama to this priest. A lengthy stay in his temple will help me to win his confidence. Perhaps I may return with treasures of untold worth."

"Is that why your mane has fallen under the scissors?"

"Yes, at least, that is one of the reasons."

"When do you leave?"

"In a few days, I hope."

"I suppose, after this, then, you will only pay flying visits to Peking?"

"Probably. Peking tires me, everything here is just a bit rotten. There are no real Chinese and the sight of all the round heads to which modern ideas have fitted that great invention of this century, the bowler, makes me sick."

"But there are not only Chinese in Peking," said Beaurelois, who thought the moment had come to speak. "The Europeans, as a community, are quite interesting and you will see the like nowhere else. You would have to search very thoroughly before discovering, in our midst, the ideas that are killing the old world."

"Perhaps, but I mistrust that legend about broad mindedness across the seas. Does no one talk scandal in Peking? Don't you take any interest in the doings of your neighbours?"

"No!"

"Well, seldom, and anyhow not maliciously," corrected Maugrais.

"Don't you people in Peking ostentatiously extend a very welcoming hand to rich scamps? Are not unknown genius and virtue as we understand them, obliged to give way to mediocrity 'en place' as we used to say?"

"You always must exaggerate," said Maugrais. "Probably we have neither great genius nor great virtues here. There are witty, well behaved and even amiable people and also people we like and others we don't...."

"And, also, there are no scamps, not even millionaire ones," said Beaurelois laughing.

"And if there were," continued Maugrais, "we have not come across them, we don't even know if they exist, or where they live if they do. Peking is a city of officials, slightly formal and perhaps a trifle snobbish, but, anyhow, clean minded and agreeable to frequent. It is a casual and temporary agglomeration of people who have seen the world, have stayed in Paris and London; passed through Florence and Athens, played with politics in Petrograd or with finance in America; people who have crossed all the seas, made collections in the East and made love in Venice. . . but it is above everything else, a city that has given birth to a special type of human being. . . the Peking silhouette."

"Of which you are a good specimen," interrupted Beaurelois.

"Not altogether." Maugrais tried to defend himself, smilingly. Then suddenly turning to Chatours, "look here, old man, what are you doing to-morrow?" And he glanced significantly at Beaurelois.

"Eating, thinking and not sleeping."

"That's not right. You must not leave this city, I can assure you, without studying the life the Europeans lead here," said Beaurelois.

"Perhaps I am wrong. What do you suggest I do?'

"Well, you can have no excuse for refusing to dine with me to-morrow night. You will meet, I am vain enough to believe, the nicest people in town and you will still be able to carry out easily that programme you have just planned for your day."

Chatours was about to attempt to invent a reason for refusing this invitation when he saw Maugrais make a sign to him to accept. In his mind he began to doubt. Beaurelois, with an understanding quite unusual in him, observed what was taking place and seized the opportunity to interpret the silence according to his own wishes.

"Its quite understood, then, isn't it? You will have lots of time when you are with your priest to cultivate your love of solitude; a little gaiety will amuse you and you need only remember as much of it as pleases you."

Chatours smiled; as a matter of fact he was flattered by the way he was being pressed. To show he considered the invitation accepted, Maugrais changed the conversation. "Tell me how goes your adventure with young Chu. I hear you met with an unexpected resistance."

Chatours looked sad, "I am afraid, my friend, this country is going to the dogs. In less than three years the Japanese will be in Peking. A country that wants a place in the sun must be able to depend on one of the two greatest forces in the world, military or moral. China has never been able to obtain the former and is beginning to lose the latter. European civilization has scarcely touched it and its own ancient civilization is rapidly dying out. Its special sort of civilization is made up of traditions, of a mass of fatalistic philosophy, of healthy morality, and of family customs. At Yukatan I saw an architect try to restore one of those monuments of the long vanished culture of the Mayas; as his work progressed, the building lost its balance; balance that was based not on mathematical calculations, but on the laws of assimilation which regulate not only the men and beasts, but the things of this world. It was useless to try to erect scaffolding or anything of that sort; this building, a hundred times centenarian, finally crumbled at the feet of the horrified American. My friends, modern Chinese are incompetent architects and they will make the magnificent structure of China which has been preserved for 40 centuries, crumble to pieces through lack of moral balance."

He went towards the door without taking leave, Maugrais stopped him with a gesture. "If I understand rightly, you are stating that China's downfall is at hand just because the daughter of the ex-minister Chu chooses to resist your advances."

Chatours paused a second, thinking, his hand on the door knob, then he said gravely, almost sadly, "That's it, you have understood," and he disappeared.

Beaurelois took out his watch. "Past one, I must take my departure too. I don't want to keep my wife waiting. I suppose that the result of our conversation is that your place will be put at our table to-morrow." He held out his hand. "And remember what I say, you are on a dangerous incline. You are too much alone, you are yielding to the debilitating air of this place. Take care you don't shortly become a Peking silhouette, one of those peculiar people who avoid Europeans like the plague and isolate themselves in a temple in the Chinese quarter, seeking, alone, the origin of some long forgotten hieroglyphics and, at nights, air their melancholy on the Tartar Wall which overlooks the yellow roofs of the Imperial City, dreaming of the barbarous and splendid past related in the Court annals. I am afraid I detect a tendency in you to become a 'Chinese-loving misanthrope' and that would be a calamity. You must pull yourself together, come out of your seclusion, see your friends, and above all..." he concluded as he went into the hall, "come to dinner to-morrow."

As soon as Maugrais found himself alone, he took a long look at the Japanese prints that decorated the smoking room walls. His glance rested on the slender distorted body of one of Utamaru's Geisha. "Her head, studded

SILHOUETTES OF PEKING

with pins, the typical head dress of the courtisan, seems like a halo of love encircling her," he said to himself, "as for her little body always bent or distorted, with neither shoulders nor hips, it appears to indicate that, mastered by man's sensuality, the musme carries through the endless ages an indissolvable alliance of pain and love. But there is a great deal of truth in Beaurelois's words and advice," he thought. "I certainly felt better when I used to get up at six, see my ponies at their training on the race course and coming home sit down to write a dispatch about the programme of the developement of the Chinese railways, with the illusion that not only would it be read, but that it might prove useful. And when I cursed my partner for his bad play at bridge in the Club in the afternoons, and when at dinner, I made love to my neighbour, who very often was not even listening to me and would reply, for instance, that she did not feel any draught, yes, I certainly felt better, both physically and morally."

He thought for an instant, then he rose. "Well, let's take up our old existence; I'll follow a programme of activities and a mode of living. I shall start my abandoned work again, that old plan for the merging of French industrial companies in China. Even if the Board of Directors of my Company don't approve of the idea, it will be astonished at my waking up. Then I shall begin to go out, to small dinner parties especially, they are less boring and the food is better. I shall play bridge at the Club again. I shall also take more exercise, riding and going for long walks on Sundays with the members of the Sunday Club, composed of the sporting elite of Peking, who, each Sunday, lunch in some temple in the Western Hills. And last but not least, I shall go home on leave in the autumn. It is strange but true that a European must sometimes return to his native air in order to get rid of the morbid germs of the East. He comes back a few months later with new blood, more ambition and fresh aspirations, all of which seem to diminish here. He comes back also with a desire to live which before he left was noticeably slight. . ."

He walked over to his desk, his mind quite made up. "Where shall we begin?" He thought for a minute, ready for the fray. "Well, let's start by dining to-morrow with the Beaurelois," and satisfied with this decision, he came back to the sofa, and lay down again on the couch, pulling towards him the cushions which had grown more supple and obedient as if overcome with reverence for this awakening energy.

SILHOUETTES OF PEKING

CHAPTER II

SEATED at her dressing table, Blanche de Beaurelois put the last touches to her hair, sticking a hairpin here and there to sustain the clever structure of golden curls that her maid had not been able to steady thoroughly.

This extremely important part of her dressing terminated, she cast a complacent glance at her mirror. The reflection it shewed apparently gratified her, for she immediately gave herself into the expert hands of the faithful Eugenie, who was waiting to slip her frock over her head.

A tardy sunbeam at the end of this June day, streamed through the wide open bay window and flooded the whole room with a soft light. It shewed up the harmonious lines of the young woman's figure. Fairly tall, full figured, hair like gold, she looked like one of those beauties Rubens loved to paint. She had already passed her thirtieth year but was still capable of holding her own; even if the sharp tongued Maxwell, the new American secretary, said, and probably rightly too, that there might be some surprises at "the unpacking", it was certainly true that Blanche looked a very desirable person and really cut out for "love's duel" as La Fontaine has it. Perhaps she was rather too free in her use of those cosmetics which are supposed to assist women in correcting the imperfections of their complexions, for she was never without a layer of paint. This gave her face an artificial brilliancy without which it would have certainly looked better.

But in this country of the colourful *Mings* should we blame a woman for brightening the natural richness of her colour, should the touching up of her face be counted as a crime against her, even if it should be done with the idea of hiding the unwanted wrinkles?

During the ten years that followed her marriage with Baron de Beaurelois, Blanche could boast of never having failed in her role of a great coquette. Soon after her marriage, she had gone to Japan, then to China, her husband being interested in the building of railways and in public works.

At Tokio first, then in Shanghai where she stayed some time, she had many adventures which amply justified the remark made about her; like nature, her heart abhorred a vacuum. Lately in Peking the place had been filled by a young Lieutenant in the British Guard who had now returned to India with his regiment.

Beaurelois was plump, rather nice looking, with upturned moustache. He always wore a selfsatisfied air which blinded him to the extent of doubting the virtue of all women except his own wife's. He was on the whole, an almost perfect type of the betrayed but sympathetic husband.

Nobody minded his conjugal misfortunes. He did not even inspire that mixture of pity and contempt that men in his case usually do. It was an understood thing that he was the husband of an unfaithful wife and for ten years, everyone whose business took them to China, recognised the situation without even thinking of emitting a criticism. After a vacation, those who returned from Europe simply asked, "by the way, with whom is the Baroness now?" Then their curiosity satisfied, sure to avoid making awkward remarks in the future, they greeted Beaurelois with pleasure and shook hands with him effusively.

And when playing bridge, even if he had one of those extraordinary no trump hands, and even when his persistent luck seemed out of the common, a less lucky opponent would scarcely take the trouble to smile at the winner.

Like happy nations, he had no history. Maybe because his temperament forbade those effusions for which his wife easily found vigorous substitutes, maybe, on the contrary, Blanche, artful when it was a question of calming any suspicion, knew how to reserve a certain share of her affection for his personal use. Whatever the reason, he never sought distraction from the humdrum monotony of his married life. On the contrary, he was most attentive to his wife and took a lot of trouble to increase the opportunities for her to meet the people she liked. No one smiled any more so accustomed were they to see the happiest of the triangle regularly make fast friends with the man who was, for the time being, Mme. de Beaurelois's choice.

Lately, Blanche had been worrying him; she was irritable for nothing, extremely nervous and had not been at all herself since the departure of the British regiment. She had even given him such frequent proofs of her affection in their moments of intimacy, that, although he was very flattered, he was not a little astonished, unused as he was to such treatment. Only the other day she had been complaining that her friends neglected her, and had led Louis up to the point of proposing this dinner party. Without seeming to touch on the subject she had mentioned Jean Maugrais's name. He had been in her mind some time now, as a possible candidate for the little lieutenant's place. It would please her to replace that sportsman by an intellectual, whose solid biceps and splendid figure promised great things for the tête-à-tête during which she meant to encourage more intimate relations later on. And great was her disappointment when she received the note refusing her invitation; she was not even satisfied at the result of her husband's visit, but happily, another last minute refusal had given her a fresh occasion for asking Maugrais to reconsider his answer and to her surprise he accepted with pleasure.

Although she was astonished that the momentary object of her desire should not show more eagerness, Blanche was now completely reassured as to the final victory. If necessary she could force his attentions, his devotion and .... the rest. The difficulties she was meeting with only enhanced the value of the prize. In short, resistance made her keener.

All these things flitted through her mind as her husband came to tell her it was time to go downstairs to receive her guests. The "boys" were waiting silently in the hall, clothed in long robes of tussore, their waists encircled by a sash with an enamelled buckle. They wore ceremonial hats of straw with red horse hair.

Young Graziolli of the customs service arrived first. He began talking at once about the various race courses in China. He was better acquainted with them than any one else because he had won a good many prizes; he was one of the best jockeys of that time. Other guests soon streamed in and finally came the beautiful Mrs. Brixton, her husband with her, though he had never even sent word that he had returned from his trip that very morning. The two women exchanged the usual politenesses with the exaggerated show of friendship always shown by two rivals to hide their real feelings.

Beaurelois, going from group to group, offered cocktails and pressed his guests to taste the sandwiches made of the yolk of egg and stuffed olives. The lady of the house began to feel uneasy; Jean Maugrais had not yet arrived. Would he desert at the last moment? No, here he was, followed closely by the Maricourts, always the last everywhere. The husband, of course, said it was his wife's fault. She got home from tennis at 8 o'clock; she always did things like that; she would never learn to be punctual.

"Now, old man," said Maugrais, annoyed at all this fuss, "don't talk nonsense, you weren't home early either, because at 8 you were still playing bridge at the Club."

The first "boy" announced dinner.

They went into the dining room, passing through the suite of drawing rooms, with their inviting divans and discreet lights.

This discretion showed that the mistress of the house was a past master in the art of flirting and knew its needs.

Beaurelois had carefully followed Maugrais' advice and put Chatours next to Mrs. Brixton. Already before they had finished the soup, the pretty American opened fire: "Is all they say about you true," she said suddenly, "I am told you live over by the Bell Tower in the Chinese City near the Wall. Your house is full of mystery, and if I am to believe all I am told, very strange things happen there."

"Good Heavens, Mrs. Brixton, people are very kind to take such an interest in me and in what I do. Of course like all good globe trotters, I ought to stay at the Hotel de Pekin, but I can assure you that nothing strange or mysterious happens in the Chinese house that shelters me. I am stupid enough to be interested in China, so naturally I avoid the Legation Quarter where my old friends the bonzes would fear to venture. I prefer my solitude to the noisy comings and goings on the scented shores of the Jade Canal, which, by the way I regret to learn is going to be transformed into a smart boulevard." This allusion to the stench of the sewer poetically named "Jade Canal" made his neighbour smile. She was on the point of continuing her questions when Jean Maugrais, who had been watching her, joined in the conversation.

"Don't believe him, Mrs. Brixton, look at him, he is just a mass of vice; he goes in for all sorts of orgies. It certainly was not for nothing that he fled from France where he had made himself quite impossible. Here he can gratify his strange appetites and satisfy all his curiosity."

He did not seem to relish the joke. Mrs. Brixton, on the contrary, her eyes shining, hastened to draw from her neighbour in an aside, some details of that life, full of mystery, therefore so exciting.

Sandwiched between two Ministers, Blanche lent only half an ear to the description of the purchase of the last batch of curios that Maricourt was giving with much satisfaction. He had discovered in a shop on Hatamen street two vases of the Ming period without a chip. Gaillard, who buys Chinese works of art for Paris houses, had guaranteed they were authentic. The price was only three hundred dollars; it was really for nothing, they must have been stolen from the Palace.

Then every one waxed enthusiastic over a duck's liver pate being handed round. Questioned about it, Blanche answered with modesty that it was made in the house. Mme. de Beaurelois boasted and rightly too, that they had the best cook in Peking. She could not resist the pleasure of recalling how, some weeks earlier, the wife of a South American Minister, newly arrived in China, had tried to get him. All the guests smiled, for the tale had already spread. The lady in question, dining at the Beaurelois, had frankly confided in her table neighbour, the Russian Minister, and expressed her surprise at the refusal she had encountered. He, without a minute's hesitation, repeated it in Russian to his neighbour, a fellow-country woman, who hastened to circulate it.

For some time the conversation turned on culinary matters. Maricourt observed that his cook had an extraordinary receipt for tournedos with a Bearnaise sauce. The French Legation had given it to him, for a certain Minister there in the Boxer time, had brought to Peking a Cordon bleu who had been trained at the Maison Doré. This led the conversation to the Legation siege and the hardships undergone, and for a few minutes an old resident was allowed to air his reminiscences.

Meanwhile, at the other end of the table, Maxwell talked politics and mourned over China's senility. In spite of the Republic, nothing was changed and the same faults were repeated. Chatours, who began to feel embarrassed at Mrs. Brixton's questioning, joined in this conversation: "I find," he said, "that it is wrong to criticize what is actually happening in China or to wish to impose on this unfortunate country our own so-called superior method of governing. On the contrary, Europe has much to learn from China. The latter was civilized long before the former. Is it not marvellous to see how this huge country is governed; its population is more than 400 millions! The number of officials is infinitesimal in comparison, so the public scarcely suffer from their unnecessary zeal.

"Although all European Powers have crushing budgets showing every year the inevitable deficit, and thus worrying the minds of those who think of the future, China, in its greater wisdom, has such a simple governing machine that it does not even feel the need of establishing its debit and credit accounts every year.

"Of course you have no taxi cabs crowding the streets, nor homicidal autobuses, that terror of the pedestrian, but are they essential to the happiness of the majority? On the other hand, see how good the police service is here, you can go anywhere without fear, at any hour of the day or night whilst in Paris even in broad day-light you may be attacked on the Boulevards by Hooligans."

This paradox amused them all and other talk ceased.

Jean Maugrais, astonished to see the unusual turn the conversation had taken, answered. "That's all very well, but you would have great difficulty in getting us to admit

the corruption that flourishes in all ranks is a thing we should envy China."

"The squeeze," said Chatours, "is certainly not the best thing in the organization of the country, but after all, it is just as good a system of government as many others. The officials buy their jobs, certainly, but then, they thus procure, directly or indirectly, important sums for the Treasury. Is it not just they should recover their expenditure by taking a percentage of the taxes they collect? The administration of China is in a way farmed out to the Mandarins, that is all. But did we not employ the same methods up to the time of the Revolution?"

"Yes," said Maugrais, "but that was the cause of the Revolution."

The women, who had been amused for a minute or two, ceased to listen.

Jean noticed this and so did Chatours, but he could not resist the pleasure of adding: "The Revolution took place here too, but it was better managed than in France, without a scaffold, without any taking of the Bastille. A simple decree from the young Emperor who, acknowledging himself unworthy to reign, took upon his shoulders the responsibility of the country's ills and declared to his people a Republic would henceforth be the form of Government in China! That sufficed to change the established order. After that, can you pretend that China is not a country of progressive ideas?"

They all laughed and the conversation fell back into the usual trend of gossip. That good sort, Graziolli, talked scandal as willingly as he told stories of ponies. He counted the women who would spend the hot season in Pei Tai Ho or Shan Hai Kwan and the young sparks who would join them there later.

The "boys" with their noiseless steps, handed round the savoury. Dinner was finished. Blanche signed to her husband and they all went on to the verandah where coffee was served. Unconsciously the party formed itself into groups. As a consolation for Maugrais' indifference, Blanche exerted herself to amuse Chatours. She showed him a Kosseu she had just bought. Mrs. Brixton, abandoned by Chatours, suddenly perceived she was near Maugrais. Having nothing to say to her, he found the situation awkward. A cold and inimical expression in her eyes astonished him. He did not want to break the silence so pretended to be listening interestedly to a dissertation on *Hans* dynasty bronzes begun by Maricourt, who liked to be considered the greatest authority on curios in Peking.

In one corner of the verandah, those whom Blanche irreverently called "the bores" talked finance and politics. Every one felt a little weary from the heat of the day. No one wanted to start a game of bridge, it was better out of doors in the fresh air.

A distant sound of brass instruments was wafted nearer by the light breeze rising. Some one suggested going on the Wall to listen to the Wagons Lits Orchestra playing that evening.

"What a good idea," exclaimed Mrs. Brixton, "up there it will be cool, don't you think so, dear," she added to Blanche, and as Maugrais approached, she turned her back on him abruptly. She took Maxwell's arm and went out.

Beaurelois rang and ordered rickshaws; soon the whole party was on its way to the slope leading to the Wall near the Water Gate.

SILHOUETTES OF PEKING

CHAPTER III

THE Baroness' guests wandered about among the decidedly mixed crowd on the Wall where white shirt fronts rubbed against more democratic clothes and against soldiers dressed in khaki. Surrounded by electric lamps, a Chinese orchestra played one of Meyerbeer's overtures. The sounds penetrated the dark night. They spread towards the vast and sombre structure of the Chienmen Gate, lost themselves near the Hatamen, whose outline was hardly visible. The flow of people was less dense as the distance from the music became greater, the promenaders slackened their pace and lowered their voices into intimate whispers. Maugrais hastened to leave the crowd. He could hardly distinguish the faces of the people he jostled and he tried to make himself unrecognizable by jamming his hat over his eyes. He wanted to dream peacefully far from the crowd, to sit on the edge of the Wall, to light a cigarette and to listen to the music from so far away that it would sound beautiful. Hardly had he gone a few steps, however, than a powerful athletic form approached. He received a friendly blow that nearly broke his collar bone. Some one bellowed like a bull: "Hello, what the devil have you been doing lately, we never see anything of you." It was the Norwegian Minister, a huge blonde, addressing him. The best sportsman in China, he spent his life playing tennis, polo and doing calisthenics in his garden, professing great contempt for all people suffering from nerves or melancholy, all poets, philosophers or epicures. "They are just riff-raff," he would say, "I would soon cure them of their fads; a good ten mile walk at 5 in the morning, a ride in the afternoons and, between times, a few calisthenics. Believe me, old man, a thirty pound dumb bell in each hand, arms outstretched for fifteen minutes, and the most stubborn hypochondriac would be cured."

"Now then, dreamer," he roared, "here all alone. Come and keep my wife company; she is over there, near the orchestra."

But Maugrais mumbled vague excuses and literally tore himself from the grasp of the powerful athlete. He always tried to avoid Mrs. Immersteht as much as possible. She was famed for her stupidity but loved to discuss serious subjects. She would look wise and ask: "What do you think of the latest political events?" or else, "I should very much like to have your opinion on the Vice-President of the Republic." Maugrais avoided her like the plague. He hurried along and was soon rid of the crowd. Now he was alone on that part of the Wall; above him, a sky studded with stars; beneath him, on both sides of the Wall the dark nocturnal city of Peking; a strange murmur rose from the immense town; distant voices mingled with the noise of heavy carts rolling over the stony road; the braying of donkeys, the cries of camels, the barking of wretched dogs wandering in and out of the Hutungs. Rising like the tide to the top of the Wall, the noise increased sometimes to such an extent that one could pick out the voice of a

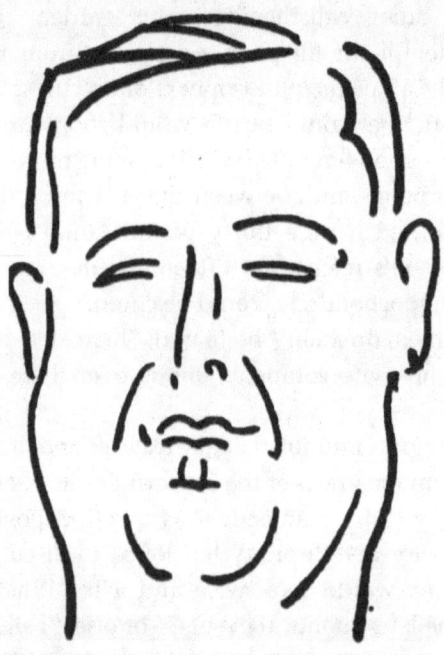

peddler calling his wares and striking a gong, or the shrill notes of a street singer, on the crumbling walls, singing of the legendary splendour of bye gone centuries. Then the noise gradually lessened like the ebbing tide, finally dying away in a confused rumour. Maugrais walked slowly now. Suddenly he heard steps behind him. Several persons seemed to be following and gaining upon him. He waited for them to pass. Two outlines appeared and stopped in front of him. He recognized Mrs. Brixton and Maxwell.

"Thank you," said the American to her escort, "you may leave us now." The young man did not even look surprised at being dismissed like that. Bowing slightly, he turned on his heel and disappeared into the night. "I saw you coming this way alone, so I followed you. Are you surprised?"

"Nothing surprises me any more," answered Maugrais.

"At least you might say you feel flattered."

"Please allow me to be silent and to offer my arm." She took it, pouting a little. After a minute, she added:

"Sometimes I don't know what to think of you; there are times when you are a mixture of great tenderness and icy coldness, of an almost insolent indifference and an attentive warmth. You did not welcome me very kindly a moment ago and now you are squeezing my bare arm as if it were the arm of your wife or mistress."

"Or my friend or sister," said Maugrais.

"What does that mean?"

"Nothing, I am only stating a fact."

She hesitated, seeming to collect her thoughts. "Yes," she said all at once. "I couldn't sleep all night after what took place between us in the blue room when Melle de Frissonges came upon us suddenly. What about you?"

"I, oh, I slept like a top." He hastened, however, to add, "but strong emotions always tire me out."

"I am afraid, yes, afraid, I know it is silly of me, but I can't help it. . . ."

"Good Heavens, of what?"

"I am afraid you will make me suffer and I don't want to suffer. I am not built for that sort of thing."

"Oh, you are quite wrong about yourself," said Maugrais gravely, "Mme. de Beaurelois, for instance, is a woman not made for suffering. She is cut out for love and passion; she gives herself wholly in a wave of abandon, of charitable feeling and self sacrifice. She is at the same time the mother and the mistress of the man she loves. She gives all she can, that is why she is happy. You, on the contrary, give nothing to the men you love; you only take from them. You are a ghoul for love, a vampire for passion. Besides, your love is simply jealousy, vice, desire and pain. Therefore, if I made you suffer, I should only be a blind tool in the hands of Fate."

They had reached the old guard house of a Manchu guard; its walls were dilapidated, there was no roof but at the back of the room, there were the remains of a Kang. Mrs. Brixton stopped for a minute; she hesitated, then she entered and sat on the wooden plank that was all that was left of the Kang. Maugrais seated himself beside her. The orchestra could no longer be heard. The couple were alone on the Wall; below them lay the immense city of Peking, the murmur of the restless town rising in the night like a long wail of distress. For some time neither spoke. Mrs. Brixton rested her head on Maugrais's shoulder and presently her lips sought his. "Jean, why do you treat me like that. Your words are cruel and sarcastic, and I, at least for to-night, am sincere and tender." Maugrais, his mouth clinging to hers, seemed about to speak when he realized she was on the point of abandoning herself. So, sure of himself and her, he gently pushed her down on to the *Kang* and with his free hand, caressed almost mechanically the firm flesh of her limbs. He could feel the delicate lace of the open work stocking that moulded her leg. She was already panting; suddenly ungluing her mouth from his, she began to whisper things to him that were in some language he

did not know, but he guessed they were both obscene and tender. At that minute, Jean raised his eyes; overhead he glimpsed the vast dark firmament, and in that distant sky baby stars shone out like a thousand timid smiles. He stared at one of those heavenly visions, and suddenly he saw it detach itself from the sky and slowly glide towards him, leaving a trail of light behind. As the star slipped towards the earth, shining brightly, Jean felt himself filled with joy, but as it gradually reached the horizon, his heart strings tightened. The star disappeared suddenly behind the Temple of Heaven, sending in a flare of light a farewell kiss. Maugrais's arms relaxed and a feeling of utter boredom overwhelmed him. He did not move, and after a few seconds that seemed like centuries, he saw two great eyes filled with astonishment and wrath fixed on him. A wave of intense fatigue swept over him and in a sudden movement he loosed the woman, and, placing his arms behind his head, lay on his back looking upwards at the sky. He fancied that he was thousands of miles from the city, and that the sounds which reached him were the rustling of the trees in an enormous forest where he dwelt as a hermit, dreaming the prehistoric dream of beasts and plants. Mrs. Brixton sat up and looked at him. She decided it would be better to laugh at this extraordinary adventure, but her laugh sounded false, a harsh discord in the stillness of the night.

"Oh so the poor thing is tired, how funny, how extremely funny."

She sought for words to wound him. "Why don't you follow Immersteht's advice and go in for a little healthy gymnastics?"

Jean did not answer, he was too tired. He hoped vaguely that she would overcome her rage. But his silence only seemed to exasperate her more. Standing up and still laughing nervously, she tried to find more offensive things to say, things that would be biting and cruel. But he lifted his head and said slowly: "In my childhood, when I did wrong or committed a sin of omission, I asked to be forgiven in these words, forgive me, I did not do it on purpose. Shall I do an act of contrition for this sin of omission?"

"If you mean you will never do it again, I can assure you of that," said Mrs. Brixton, "at least not with me. But, that will do, give me your arm and let us join the Baroness." The journey back was dreary. The American walked quickly; there seemed something firm and resolute in her step. Maugrais thought of his smoking room and his library. He cursed his stupidity for having been led into accepting this dinner party. They approached the orchestra and as the sounds of the music drew nearer and the crowd thickened, Mrs. Brixton seemed to unbend. When they reached the gaily lighted esplanade, she even went so far as to make some amiable remark.

"Thank you," she said to Maugrais, taking her hand from his arm and loud enough to be heard by every one. "You have been very amusing to-night, very amusing indeed."

"I did my best, Mrs. Brixton," he answered.

"I noticed it," she retorted, her eyes flashing suddenly. A few minutes later they were in the midst of their friends.

The Argentina Minister approached. He was small, refined looking, elegant but melancholy.

"How boring it is here," he said, "this is the first time I have been here this year, and it is certainly the last."

"That's not very nice to us," said Baroness de Beaurelois.

"Oh I appreciate your company but I dislike this crowd, this hubbub, this infernal music. Wait, though, I have an idea," and coming close to the Baroness he whispered a few words in her ear. She laughed and drawing him aside, they began to conspire. Seizing the opportunity Maugrais moved quietly away and looked over the gap in the Wall towards Chien Men Station and the Chinese city. He perceived that, unfortunately, he was not alone. Standing a few feet from him was the slender figure of a woman who seemed to be watching the movements in the station. He began to move away so as not to disturb the solitary dreamer when he heard a well known voice call him.

"It's you, Monsieur Maugrais, I recognized you in spite of the darkness." And the figure came towards him; it was Melle de Frissonges.

"Whatever are you doing here all alone, where are all your admirers. Queen, where is your Court?"

"I have left them. If you only realized how they bore me, all of them." There was a note of bitterness in her voice, almost a sound of despair.

"Good heavens, what has happened? Since when this disillusion?"

"Since when? Always. They are so stupid, all those people, they are so boring they send me to sleep." Maugrais looked at her; he was surprised at her attitude. She leant on the gap in the Wall, her form bent like a young reed and her heavy blonde hair waving in the wind. Her long bare arm against her dark frock seemed like a broken twig hanging from a black tree trunk. "Now then," he said, "you were certainly not bored at dinner to-night. I heard Maxwell telling you some shocking stories that were strong enough to make a trooper blush."

"Yes, and I even laughed so as not to show that I had already heard the story. Young Vladowsky told it to me last night at the Russian Legation."

"But after dinner I saw. . . . ."

"After dinner Graziolli, pretending to show me a new Italian dance, put his arm round my waist and manoeuvred his legs in the most astonishing way. At first I let him continue because I didn't care what he did, but when I saw it was going to last too long, I made him stop and sent him away telling him he didn't know how to dance."

"But if all that does not amuse you, why do you go out into society?"

Melle de Frissonges looked at him out of her great black eyes.

"What else is there in Peking for a girl to do? If we lived in France, I should still be at school, I should have friends of my own age, interesting books, music, — oh, I forgot, we are at a concert now — the theatre, in fact all the amusements one gets in Europe. And above all I should have something I haven't got here, something I may never get."

"What is it?"

"I don't know if I should tell you, I am afraid you may not understand." For a few minutes she was silent, then in a soft monotonous tone, she continued: "I was twelve when my father went to France on leave and took me with him. It was my first visit to what should be my native land; you know I was born in Korea at the Pi Yang mines. For eight months we lived with my uncle in Provence, it was a revelation to me. The gay, cheerful landscape fascinated me immediately. How could that strong, healthy nature be compared with the washed out places in Japan, the savage sadness of Korea, haunted as it is with the white spectres of the natives, or even with the wild beauty of China speaking of death and memories? I was so fascinated that I had to be torn away by force, but I brought back with me buried in the bottom of my heart a vision of Europe. . . From my windows I could see the green fields through which ran a silver stream and where an old wind mill turned patiently. Opposite there was the dark line of the sea; behind, cottages which shewed white in the sunshine. To the left and right on the horizon, the Alps, laden with years, stood out." She turned towards Maugrais and her voice grew stronger, "I hate Peking, China, the Far East and I am not at all in the swim here. Oh if only I could live in France in the country far from the world, if I could wander bare footed in the fresh grass and bathe in the clear water of a stream."

The young man looked at her, at a loss what to answer. He was astonished at this burst of passionate love for a country she hardly knew. But he felt he must defend the ancient land of China. However she silenced him immediately. "Tell me, have you read Kipling? You must know his theory on the Call of the East. Well, what surprises me is that no one has replied to this painful call with the urgent call of the West." She stiffened and looked wildly into the night. "You are all contaminated by the depressing and morbid atmosphere of the East and you will all be victims of it if you do not listen to the call of Europe, the call of the West which you persist in stifling."

Suddenly they saw a shadow detach itself from the crowd and approach them discreetly. "Leave me now," said Melle de Frissonges, "there comes Vladowsky to tell me he desires me without caring for me, that he wants me without being in love with me. Leave us alone, we will continue this conversation another time if you wish but I must ask you not to mention it to anyone."

"Very well," answered Maugrais gravely, as he left her. The next minute he was among his friends, Mrs. Brixton, Baroness de Beaurelois, the Argentina Minister and Chatours were all there.

"These ladies have promised to come home with me for a while to drink champagne and to smoke a few pipes, while their husbands finish discussing the fate of China to the soothing accompaniment of this orchestra. Will you join us?" Maugrais, who appreciated Count de Cordoba's refined taste and distinguished manners, accepted, and they started on their way down the slope.

"This way," said the Count, "we need not follow the Jade Canal; I am taking you to the native city. We are going to my bachelor quarters, not to the Legation. We go through the Sino-Bulgar Bank garden; the manager is a very busy man, so he lives in a temple three miles from town. Therefore he is not at home just now and we shorten our journey considerably."

They all got into rickshaws and quickly crossed Legation Quarter. Reaching the Tartar City, they passed through the dark hutungs where the wheels of their vehicles sunk into the mud and branches of huge trees overhanging the gutters brushed against their faces. The streets were empty; only solitary hawkers passed occasionally, swaying as they went, carrying baskets suspended from bamboo poles, and crying their wares before the closed doors. Here and there, very high up, above the roofs, red lanterns, the sign of bath houses, shone through the night like eyes of fire. After two or three turnings, the rickshaws stopped before a small door in a wall. The Count alighted and struck the bell, a kind of metal slab hanging in the centre of the panel. An old porter opened the door. Crossing two small courtyards, flanked

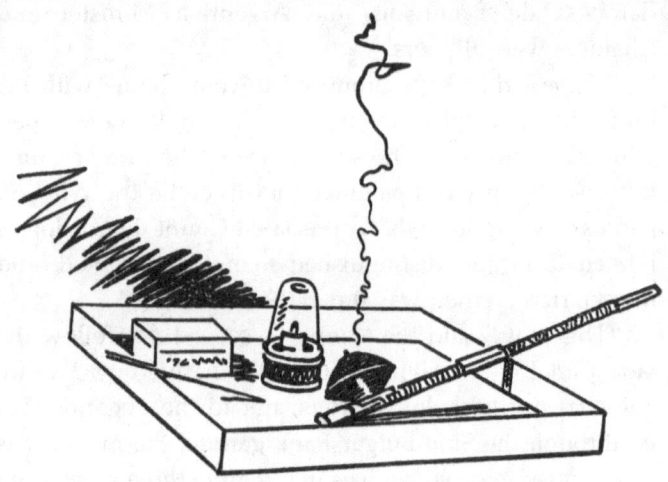

by Chinese pavilions and surrounded by stonebordered flower-beds whence escaped the scent of invisible flowers, the procession penetrated a large sheltered pavilion and entered first a vast room. The ceiling was painted with medallions representing the dragon, symbol of the astral world; shades of green, blue and red were intermingled. Large pillars, also multicoloured, supported this high ceiling. The room was furnished partly in Chinese, partly in European style. English furniture stood beside Cantonese blackwood chairs, a Yunnan stone inlaid in the backs of the latter. The veins of these stones recalled the ranges of mountains and the rush of the waterfalls. Japanese kakemonos hung from the walls; Kosseu screens hid the corners of the room and an old Buhl clock ornamented the mantel piece which was covered with yellow tiles taken from the Imperial Palaces. But the Count did not linger here; he led his visitors through a low door into the next room. It was smaller, and was long rather than broad; the carpet-hung walls were covered with the rich colours of Asia Minor, the beautiful Persian tints and the velvety shades of the Bokhara; numerous cushions lay about the floor which was spread with skins of all kinds. At the far end of the room, there was a very broad Turkish divan; here and there, on all the tables and stands were Chinese vases and near the divan a Korean chest had been transformed into a book case filled with specially chosen richly bound books. The chamber was lit with candles in lanterns hanging from the ceiling. A huge gilt and lacquered Buddha seated on a lotus flower occupied one corner, a silent witness of the useless torments and perishable pleasures of mankind. Its right hand pointed to the floor, its left arm was raised to Heaven, a twofold gesture symbolizing the Hermetic Mystery.

"Sit down, on the couches, on the cushions, anywhere, please. I have ordered champagne and the pipes are almost ready." A slender boy, pale and elegant brought in a tray with glasses, a bottle of Brut Imperial and a strange looking flask. Then he vanished.

"He won't return unless we call him," said the Minister. "Here are my pages." As he spoke, the door opened and two young boys entered. They were about fifteen or sixteen years of age and wore pigtails and were dressed in long white tunics. One carried three opium pipes and the other had two small trays on which were all the necessary utensils. One of the boys sat down on the divan, the small trays in front of him. The other boy slid on to the rug. Without a word, they commenced their task with slow, traditional gestures. On the point of a long needle, they drew a piece of soft brown paste out of an ivory box. This they held over the flame of the lamp, a dark ball formed immediately. It wriggled and swelled and stretched itself towards the flame; with a deft movement it was withdrawn and kneaded in the palm of the hand or against the bowl of the pipe and again held to the flame. A drop like a black baroque pearl bubbled up seeming to attempt to throw itself into the fire, but, at the last minute, it was snatched away, softened and kneaded once more. It became docile, roasting on the point of the needle; it made a gentle sizzling sound and a strange smell like burnt cream and stale drugs filled the room.

"I must thank you for your silence, friends," said the Count, "I am convinced you felt that the moment of the preparation of a first pipe is a solemn one and should not be profaned by vain speeches. The pipes are now ready. Will the ladies do me the favour of beginning?" After a little fuss for the form, Mrs. Brixton, lying on the divan, started to inhale the heavenly drug. The boy, probably the elder of the two, served her. He looked grave and sad; his eyes were the eyes of a dreamer; his hands were slender and transparent and he looked like the prince of an Eastern Tale.

Ensconced among the cushions on the rug, the Baroness was being waited upon by the younger boy. His face was roguish, but he appeared malleable; his admirable white teeth laughed, while his sophisticated eyes respectfully watched the boiling of the black ball. The women smoked badly, they allowed the opium to burn; they blew down the pipe, blocking the narrow tube, and prevented the air from passing. Patiently and with slow gestures, the boys thrust their needle through the obstruction and offered the newly prepared pipes to the women, who, bending over the lamp, continued to inhale the poison. The men's turn came. Chatours smoked furiously, as if he wanted to swallow the bamboo pipe as well as the smoke. Maugrais smoked in silence, more expert than one would have imagined. The Minister took a pipe too, it was a plain bamboo, old and ugly, without any embellishments, very large and coloured by the smoke. The bowl, instead of being of porcelain or enamel, was of terra cotta. The Minister settled his slight body among the cushions, his ugly pipe between his fingers. He hesitated as if in secret communion with it. Then, raising it to his lips, he proceeded to inhale its contents without removing it and a few minutes afterwards he took another pipe. Impassively he collected his thoughts and fixed his sad wide-open eyes on the dark face of the Buddha opposite him. Maugrais looked at him and was struck by the resemblance between the vacant stare of the Count and the deep unfathomable look with which the Buddha contemplated humanity through a million cycles. Some time after, Cordobas rose and offered champagne, biscuits and a strange liqueur whose name he did not mention, but which sparkled in the mouth and scattered a series of strange sensations through the imbiber. The boys distributed more pipes and the real business of opium smoking began. Chatours appeared to float in an atmosphere of happiness. His tongue became loosened; he smoked, talked and drank. He passed his hand over the boys' pigtails. Maugrais took a volume of Baudelaire and read *The invitation to travel*. "My child, my sister, think of the sweetness of living there together, to love at leisure, to love and to die, in the country that looks like you."

"Oh, travel, travel," he said, throwing down the book. "To leave one country and go to an unknown one is certainly one of the greatest pleasures in life. To travel through tropical countries, live with nature, to learn about strange human races, to seek new horizons and to die, one day, in an unknown land. What can compare to the feelings of anguish and flaming hope which we have when the boat hoists its anchor and starts on its way across the seas. Mallarmé says it so well: 'the flesh is sad, alas, and I have read every book. Let us fly over there, let us fly, I feel all the birds are drunk with the foam of unknown seas and the skies.' "

Little by little, the opium made him drunk; his dilated pupils made him look like a prophet and he rambled on . . . "Oft at night lying on my matting, I have visions. I see myself dying under unknown skies. Under a torrid midday sun, a palm tree spreading its branches over me, I see myself lying there on bare white stones and dying of thirst and of lassitude. A few feet away, black and beautiful as the God Krishna, a native, swaying his body rhythmically, draws sad sounds from a thin reed. From his sphinx-like eyes, I drink the poison which kills more surely than the venom of a snake; already a heavy drowsiness creeps over me and vanquished, I roll slowly down into the darkness, my eyes turned upwards to the tropical skies."

The Count bent down to Baroness de Beaurelois and addressed her in gentle tender tones. The Baroness, slightly drunk, burnt visibly with passion and loving kindness. She seemed to offer herself with every movement, to give herself unreservedly with each word she spoke. The Count looked at her out of his good, kind eyes and treated her as a child to be coaxed. Mrs. Brixton had finished her pipe and was quietly sitting on the divan. Maugrais, turning suddenly, found himself looking right into her eyes. He shivered slightly, her gaze was so charged with blunt hate, with violence and passion. She looked at him without moving a muscle, then all at once she spoke, "Come here." He came nearer. She fixed her eyes on him for some time, his mouth, his forehead, his eyes, his hair, all arrested her attention. There was something penetrating and acute in her gaze. Mentally Maugrais compared it to the needle which was used for holding the opium to the blaze. In a hoarse voice she said, "If I were to fall at your feet, in front of every one here, if I kissed your knees, if I begged you to love me during perhaps only one second of your life, if I give up my husband, my family, all other men and even God in Whom, in spite of everything, I still believe, tell me, could you love me?" As she slowly pronounced these words, savage hate gleamed from her eyes and streamed in fiery torrents from her mouth. In spite of himself Maugrais could not help admiring her and therefore he said "No".

"Very well," and she smiled a smile that was triumphant though deathly. Then she lay back on the divan and said no more for the rest of the evening.

The Baroness floating in a sea of love and kindness, her dress open, her beautiful bosom bare, said to the Count

"No, my friend, I am afraid of growing old, afraid of the old age of ugliness and death. I want to live, to love, to bestow myself endlessly, to be born again, to live again, to bestow myself on the whole world."

"You will be born again and live anew," said the Count gravely, "for death does not exist."

"I know," said the Baroness, "but I, myself, my own personality, I , Baroness de Beaurelois, my faults and my virtues, my pet vices, I, my hands, feet, breasts and hair will disappear."

Suddenly she came nearer.

"I must tell you a dream I had last week. I came home very tired from the Italian Legation and immediately fell asleep. I saw myself as a little girl, of thirteen years of age. Looking at the water of the canal which goes into the sea, I took a paper boat from my brother's hands, my brother who was killed in the brush. I placed the little boat on the water and followed its movements with my eyes. Then I heard a window open behind me and the voice of my mother who has been dead for ten years calling to me. I sprang up to go to her when suddenly my eyes opened and I saw opposite my bed, my porcelain Koanyin cold and white. I cried silently for a long time in the lonely night and my pillow was wet with tears."

The Baroness said no more, her eyes were moist and her beautiful bare bosom heaved, the rosy tips of her breasts pointing up towards the painted ceiling. The Count turned to her and said slowly "Baroness, why should you not be a little girl of 13 playing on the edge of the canal, falling asleep on the grass and dreaming you are grown up, have married and live in a distant country."

"Now, Count, you are laughing at me."

"No, listen to me. Our celebrated Spanish poet Calderon de la Barca says: 'Life is a dream'. If Calderon had been an initiated person as well as a great author, he would have said, 'Life is a dream within a dream'."

The Baroness glanced at him questioningly.

"Don't ask me anything more, I must beg you to allow me to add nothing."

A long silence followed. The Count rose; he took a pipe and lay down at the further end of the room. He smoked for some time without a word. When he had finished he placed a transparent, weary hand on the dark head of the younger lad. The emeralds in his rings sparkled in the semi darkness and seemed to form a crown on the adolescent's forehead.

Chatours lay down besides the Baroness and presently his head was on her kindly knees. He seemed to be saying passionate and tender words to her. She listened dreamily, her fingers lingering caressingly on the young man's hair. On her lips played the smile of a woman who knows that much will be forgiven her for she has loved much. Suddenly Mrs. Brixton rose, declared it was past midnight and their husbands on the wall must certainly have noticed their absence by then. The Baroness who never hesitated to tell fibs, exclaimed, "All right, we will tell them we went to the Wagons Lits Hotel to drink a glass of champagne and to see the famous Iko Lang Tang."

Her troubles already forgotten, she got to her feet, pulled her frock up over her shoulders and laughed, showing all her beautiful strong teeth which were made for cracking nuts and her full red lips which were certainly made for kisses.

They took leave of their amiable host. He went as far as the door with them, accompanied by his silent pages. The women got into rickshaws and Chatours asked if he might see the Baroness safely home, but at the last moment, probably mistaking the way, he took her in a totally different direction. It was noticed by all of them, but no one took the trouble to remark upon what was in reality quite unimportant.

The Count found himself alone. The air was warm, the night calm and dark. He placed his right hand on the head of his younger page and said, "They have all gone, I am glad to be alone, the world is too noisy. I like you, my child, because you are quiet. Women are talkative and expansive in love, my dream is spoilt by their unrest, the charm is broken — broken by their sighs, their caresses, their transports — their egoism. You at least know how to remain silent while I love; you have grasped a mystery no woman will ever understand as long as this world exists; you understand the subject of our love is but a lucky chance, an inevitable necessity for the love dream of our soul." He shut the door and vanished.

Maugrais walked all alone down the deserted Hutung. A street hawker passed, probably the last for that night. He gave a shrill cry as if to awaken all that drowsy atmosphere. A rickshaw coolie dozed under the wall. The swelling murmur of the City had ceased; Peking was now asleep. Suddenly at the corner of the Hutung at a cross road, Maugrais saw a strange figure waiting. He stopped short and recognized Mr. Brixton. He was not tall, but squarely built and very British. The husband of the beautiful American stood motionless, in a white dinner jacket smoking a long cigar. He did not

evince the slightest surprise at the sight of Maugrais. "Hullo," he said, "what a beautiful night." Maugrais grasped that Brixton had in all probability seen his wife pass in a rickshaw. He surmised also that the Englishman was trying to make sure if she really was at Count de Cordobas' house. All these ideas and many others flashed through his brain. Nevertheless he appeared as indifferent as Brixton.

"Yes, a lovely night, the music bored you I suppose, so you strolled through the Chinese city. I quite agree it is more interesting."

Brixton made no reply. They continued their way together in silence, going in the direction of the Legation Quarter. Maugrais thought he noticed Brixton sometimes cast discreet though sharp glances at him and imagined the other suspected him of being his wife's lover. That idea and the stubborn silence of the Englishman suddenly made him furious. He turned to Brixton and said abruptly in an unamiable tone, "Well what are you thinking about like that?" Brixton turned his clean shaven face towards the speaker, took his cigar from between his lips and answered slowly. "I , I was thinking of a naive amusing incident of my school days. We had a school fellow called Bennett. His parents were rich and always gave him an excellent lunch to bring to school. He arrived with a small parcel of smoked herrings cheese, fruit, nuts and jam. As we had our lunch at midday during the third recreation, we amused ourselves by opening his desk during the first and second recreations and sneaking his dainties. He noticed nothing and ate what ever we left him. This continued for some months. But one day whether the things were better than usual or whether our appetites were keener I do not know, but we ate up everything and left him nothing for his lunch. At noon, when he opened his desk, he hesitated a minute at the empty drawer then closed it without a word. The next day he brought a key, locked his desk after placing his lunch within. That day his dainty meal looked more tempting than ever, but we no longer had any chance of tasting his fruit and jams." He said no more.

Maugrais had no idea what to say. However, he was thinking about answering when Brixton threw away his cigar, got into a rickshaw, raised his hat and was carried off in the direction of the Legation Quarter. Once more Maugrais found himself alone. He walked on for some time, picking his way through the mud in the Hutungs. Suddenly at a corner he perceived a caravan of camels approaching. One of the animals had a softly clanging bell round its neck.

Some coolies slept lying face downwards flat on the saddles, their heads hanging over the skinny ribs. The long string passed, majestically swaying, going towards the West to the Gobi Desert. The sound of the bell which rang gravely through the night seemed to call in an inviting and intimate way — a reminder of immense green steppes, of dry deserts, of golden sands and wide horizons bathed in the blue light.

"They are going towards the West, towards Mongolia," he said to himself. And all at once a slender figure, with long white arms rose to his mind, and anguished words sounded in his ears. "The Call of the West, the call of Europe. It is too late." He said aloud, "Already too late." Then a moment after, "But is it really too late?"

SILHOUETTES OF PEKING

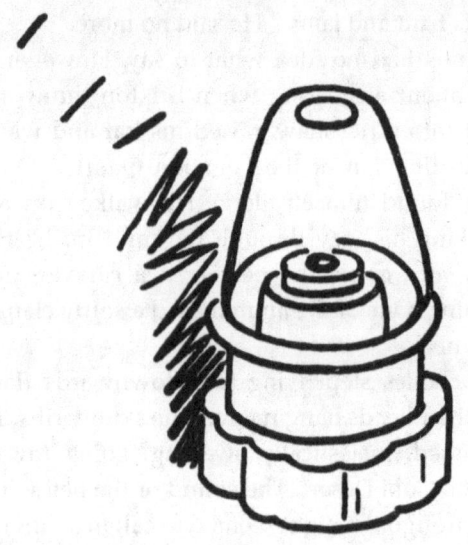

CHAPTER IV

"DEAREST one, The memory of the other night still lingers with me. Wait for me at your house. Blanche." Said the little note on blue paper. Chatours read it over complacently, his eyes slightly vacant.

It was a hot muggy afternoon. Out of doors the heavy, scorching air impeded one's breathing. In his little Chinese house with its small courtyards full of carefully tended rose trees, Chatours scantily clad in a silken kimono, waited dreamily, stretched full length on a large divan.

He reviewed in his mind that mad evening, that dinner he had been more or less forced to accept, the music, the soft night, the dreams in the smoking den and the final abandon of that desirable woman who perhaps only under the influence of the heavenly drug, had on that very first evening, given him exactly what he desired with the very words he wished for. And he had found himself very far away; very near the West. Seeker of shades and memories, in Blanche he had recognized a much loved phantom who haunted his nights and whom in spite of his exile he could not forget. It flashed through his mind he might be able to love again, he might find himself in that lost frame of mind he had so often sought in vain. And as he waited now for Blanche, the wish to be sure of his feelings made him delightfully anxious. Would he be disappointed? He passed in review his life as he lay on the golden silk of the soft divan. He saw once more his father's house where he been reared too carefully, too gently. He pictured the Castle towers, the vine-covered chapel, so purple in autumn, the French garden, the espaliers where, as a child, he had stolen fruit, the familiar fields and the landscape from the terrace, where, on the horizon, one glimpsed the intense blue of the far-off sea. He thought of his dear Brittany, which had filled his soul with overmuch melancholy and his heart with some of life's weariness.

"My college days," he murmured, "how far off they seem." And he thought of his youthful dream of the time when he should understand everything, should taste of everything, when he loved life for what it hid from him, for all the curiosity it aroused in him. His thoughts passed on to the rare sensations he had gone through during his lengthy travels, to the adventures he had had in all parts of the world, the conquests he owed to his youth. He thought, too, of that particular adventure in which he had left behind a little of himself, from which he had been obliged to flee and to come to the blue city, the far-off mysterious Peking, in order to forget.

He was dreaming, a far-away look in his eyes. The cries of the Chinese city reached his ears, the cry of the street hawker, sometimes sad and monotonous, sometimes discordant and harsh; the rickshaw bells, the squeak of the water carts and the sounds of a blind man's guitar dying away in the cool closed chamber to the murmur of the electric fan.

Then he began to think of Blanche.

"Suppose I really loved her," he said. "No, that is impossible, she could not be sufficiently mine, she would never abandon herself completely enough. She is so very frivolous. So we must just amuse ourselves." And he inhaled his cigarette and tried to blow rings. They rose slowly, at first blue but ending in scented grey smoke. "No," he went on, "she is not young enough for me to fashion to my liking and her character is not supple enough for me to love her as I would like to love."

At that moment, the door-bell rang, interrupting his reverie. Chatours' heart beat faster; he rose to receive his expected visitor. High heels sounded on the stones outside, a frock rustled. In a rush of heat, Blanche entered the room. Bewildered, she leant against the wall. "Oh, hold me, dear, please, I am dazzled by the sun light and can see nothing yet. Oh, that fan is deliciously cooling. I feel better already. How charming this room is."

Then with a slight blush of modesty, "But it was not here I came the other night."

"No, dear, you are right, this room is cosier, don't you think so? Do take off your hat and make yourself at home.

You will find powder and whatever you need, even a kimono if you are too warm, in the dressing room."

"All that one can possibly want, you monster, I think I am going to be jealous," she said, going towards the small dressing room hidden behind a silken curtain. Chatours soon heard the rattle of crystal flasks. A few minutes later she returned, her arms raised as she arranged her hair, displaying her admirable bust and the pure, slender lines of her body. She had clad herself in a lavender blue kimono. Great branches of maple were painted on it, the red leaves seeming to be bleeding to death against the blue of an autumn sky.

"Come and sit down," said Chatours as he gently pushed her on to the golden cushions of the divan. The room was small, the daylight, dimmed already by the lowered mat blinds outside, filtered through the paper and shewed up the curious patterns of the wood window-sashes against the silk curtains. The whole room was blue, from the carpets to the hangings on the walls. Chinese vases made a vivid spot of colour among the strange furniture.

Old porcelain rice bowls full of flowers lay on stands and the mahogany tables were loaded with pipes, lamps, opium jars in all colours and sizes. A few photographs of friends, comrades and relatives, scattered about acted as a reminder of the West. The fan blew on a large white bowl full of ice, refreshing the air pleasantly.

"When you arrived I was thinking," said Chatours, "I was wondering if I loved you, if I could love you, or if it was only the madness of a night that gave us the illusion of love." Her eyes shining, Blanche turned gently to him. She was rather astonished at this style of speech, for she

SILHOUETTES OF PEKING

was used to mad words of tenderness and to the stalish compliments of an ordinary adventure. What did this doubt in the midst of their passion signify? How should she take such a beginning?

"Whatever do you mean, dear, illusion of love. Is it illusion when we are just the two of us and have given proof of our sentiments. What sensations are you seeking and what more can you expect?" Chatours smiled. He gave that ugly and contemptuous curl to his lips at which he was such an adept, but replied tenderly.

"My little Blanche, you do not understand . . . ."

"Do you take me for a goose?"

"No, dear, but listen to me for a moment. What would you think of a man who in matters of love is not only seeking a partner in the game but also and principally a kindred soul. Would you understand a man who seeks, in the woman to whom he is devoting himself, a little of his own mind? You must understand that such a man could only love if the woman is a mirror in which he finds his reflection, if the same feelings thrill her and if she has more or less the same ideas. She must bring her intelligence to help him and avoid any note of discord in the union of two hearts."

"But such a man would be a coxcomb, a conceited ass, who simply wanted a slave."

"A conceited ass, no, dear, an egoist, yes, who seeks in love his own satisfaction, who, by giving himself utterly, will not allow himself to be robbed. This man I have imagined is very sure of himself, and his chief satisfaction, don't you think, would be to mould a being into the image of his own soul." Chatours felt she still did not understand;

a bird of adventure, a simple small-brained soul, she could not be expected to understand.

"But why complicate life," she said, "when it is so easy to be happy and to profit by each hour without self-analysis. My dear, don't think so much. This airing of your peculiar theories has given you a care-worn look and I don't recognize in you the tender lover of the other evening. Let us be happy and banish this foolish mood. Life is pleasant, let us seize our opportunity." She drew nearer, caressing and affectionate. Chatours pressed her to him, down among the cushions. She put her head against his heart and he kissed her golden hair softly. Blanche vibrated, she pressed closer, murmuring tender words.

"Perhaps you are right, dear," he said, moved, in spite of the fading of his dream, by the perfume emanating from her, by the feelings this woman raised in him by her touching abandon. He opened her kimono tenderly. Her firm flesh seemed to breathe of passion, the colour of her hair blended with the gold cushions. The multi-coloured porcelains brightened the shadows, a Buddha sneered from his corner, the tuberoses gave forth their oppressive scent, a cicada's note sounded. In the atmosphere of that small room Blanche and Chatours, their lips joined, felt themselves yielding gently to the ardour of their senses.

At the red door of Chatours' house, in the heat, Maugrais waited for the boy to open to him. A fat porter came out at length, he bowed in the old fashioned way and bade the visitor enter. As they crossed the shady little flowery courtyard, the porter questioned the guest about his health and about his last meal. When they reached the pavilion, he took his leave with dignity, satisfied with the answers he had received. Maugrais entered the room and perceived, not without some astonishment, that the master of the house was not alone; beside him, on the sofa, clad in a blue kimono, Blanche de Beaurelois, her bare arms raised like the two handles of a jar, was putting some rebellious hairpins back into her blonde hair. His face betrayed no surprise; with an exquisite courtesy he simply shook hands with his slightly embarrassed friend and kissed Blanche's two plump arms which took a rosy hue in their confusion.

"I came to see that *Sung* painting you boasted of yesterday at the Wolf's," he explained at once. "What a good idea to put on kimonos. This hot afternoon is really terrible. If I hadn't a date in an hour, I would have done the same. You see, Madame," he continued turning to Blanche, "I am becoming a serious person, almost a business man."

The Baroness, having recovered from her momentary confusion, laughed. From Maugrais' words and attitude she recognized in him the friend who would never betray, the ally who understood and therefore sympathised, the man who pardoned because he too had suffered. "Oh yes," she retorted, her eyes brightening. "I know you have entirely changed these last few weeks. You work in the mornings, you ride in the afternoon at 5, you are even seen at dinner parties and the other evening you actually went to the cinema. It is strange, one is apt to jump to the conclusion that you are trying to lose yourself in a fever of activity and in the whirl of social life."

Maugrais smiled, he did not answer but began to look for the painting he had come to see.

"Here it is," said Chatours triumphantly, shewing a long roll of silk hanging from the wall behind a blackwood table full of bronze and plaster figures. The colouring was soft and slightly faded, the drawing a little hazy, but the subject did not lack elegance nor the unexpected.

Maugrais looked at it for some time. "Yes, may be it is a *Sung*, but I am inclined to believe it to be a *Yuan*. Anyhow it is a beautiful purchase."

"I don't like Chinese paintings," declared Blanche standing up behind Maugrais. I always like to know what a picture represents and I never can understand the Chinese subjects."

"I think I might be able to explain the meaning of this one," said Maugrais. "It is a fairly well-known legend. Here you have the inside of a Taoist temple. Buddhism was not popular in those days. Two friends are visiting an old priest and are conversing with him in the shade of the sanctuary. One approaches a wall and looks attentively at an old picture hanging on it. It represents the square before a temple. There are young people on the steps of the building. He looks at a young girl in a long golden tunic and falls in love with the chaste expression of her features. Standing in front of the picture, he looks at her and suddenly a violent sensation assails him. He is dazed, but when he recovers he sees the maiden approaching. She takes his hand, leads him into the temple to an isolated part where along walls covered with paintings and old parchments, plaster statues of the great apostles of the Tao philosophy are set out. There are also the mysterious *Kuo* instruments for the aid of divination . . . 'Live here with me,' says the priestess, and her voice was like celestial music. 'Practise silence and inactivity, two virtues symbolised eternally by Heaven and Earth. Take your fill of *Sheng*, that reviving fluid which impregnates the world and become *Sheng* yourself'."

"She spoke. He drank in her words his ears open to the wisdom that fell from her lips, whilst outside, months, even years passed by. But one day a terrible noise broke the religious silence of the sanctuary. A jealous priest, followed by an armed horde, violated the holy place to kill the intruder. Opening a secret door, the maiden led him through an underground passage and suddenly disappeared. The young man felt a great shock, and when he recovered his senses, he found himself before the picture. His friend had finished speaking with the priest, who was regarding him paternally. 'Where am I,' he stammered, 'What has happened to me?' The priest took his hand and said calmly, 'Nothing at all, a too intense current of *Tao* fluid bewildered you. It went to your head, now you are all right again.' This picture represents the moment of the young man's awakening. We may gather this experience turned him into a good neophyte, a *Shi* of the Holy doctrine of *Laotzu*."

Maugrais left the picture and examined a Satsuma incense burner representing a sleeping cat. "That story you have just told us is really beautiful," sighed Blanche, "but are you sure that it is the subject of the picture?"

"No," answered Maugrais gravely, "but that is of no importance."

"How funny you are," laughed Blanche. Tell me, is that how you amuse little Miss de Frissonges when you take her for long rides round Peking?" Maugrais coloured slightly, like a school boy found out, and went towards the door a little embarrassed.

"Oh no, we practise the cardinal virtue of the Taoist, *silence*." But Blanche once started, insisted. "Come now, I saw you the other day at the Russian Legation. You were so deep in conversation that you never even turned your head in my direction. As soon as you catch sight of her at a dinner or a tea you take shelter by her side."

And as Maugrais, still smiling, bowed a little stiffly and opened the door, she threw after him these words, perhaps prompted by her instinct of grande amoureuse, "All right, I know why you never leave Melle de Frissonges any more." Maugrais stopped short at the door and waited. "Because you are afraid of the Other." And she burst into a hearty laugh that he could still hear ringing in his ears, as he crossed the small courtyard, covered with a *pang* where the flowers, drooping in the heat, gave out only a feeble and rather morbid perfume.

SILHOUETTES OF PEKING

CHAPTER V

THE clock on the Hong Kong Bank had just struck three. Jean finished putting on his riding things. He reckoned he had fully a quarter of an hour before Melle de Frissonges was due, so he did not hurry. Pacing his room he cast a glance at the mirror and made a face. His sloppy coat was badly cut, his breeches did not fit sufficiently snug at the knee and wrinkled, his brown leather boots, too broad in the instep, did not mould his calf. His last pair from Europe was worn out long ago and they were a badly copied pair, as could easily be seen, made by a Japanese boot maker in Hatamen Street.

"After all," he thought, "we all get like that after five or six years in Peking. Every one knows I am no longer a *griffin*. Besides, no one remembers what the chic anglais is any more. Maybe my little Chinese tailor and his cut are criticized, but what do I care?" However, he could not help recalling the time when, as a smart horseman, he used to prance down the Avenue du Bois; he thought of Paris on a beautiful spring morning; the Avenue des Acacias full of people. He used to ride his handsome chestnut slowly along the road towards the pigeon shooting, recognizing, here and there among the crowd, friends with whom he amused himself and friendly faces he bowed to as he passed. How far away it all seemed. He certainly had loved his life in Paris. It had been the artificial life of pleasure that most of the young men of his age led but all the same it had pleased him. He appreciated the wit of the theatres on the Boulevards, he adored supper parties at the Pré Catalan and expeditions to Montmartre in gay society. The excursions by motor on the lovely roads through Brittany and Normandy, the flying visits to fashionable sea-side resorts during the summer months had amused him. He had enjoyed being a part of the crowd hungry for pleasure, for whom life was an eternal carnival and whose sole occupation seemed to be seeking amusement.

However, he was blasé and skeptical, and could not content himself with simply watching amusedly all these puppets. He delighted in trying to discover people's real feelings under their masks.

He had found keen enjoyment in studying the activities of what is commonly known as *la vie parisienne*. Frequenting actors, an ardent first-night goer, in touch with the best known journalists, hearing the gossip those politicians who haunt the boulevard restaurants love to spread, he felt he was really living the slightly superficial though intense life usually led by the true Parisian, though, in reality, he was only studying the habits and customs.

But after a few seasons, this brilliant but monotonous life had finished by boring him; little by little he had tired of always discovering the same type with different features. A liaison which dragged on, while neither would own that the great passion had gradually changed to indifference, was the climax. He found it impossible to continue the life he was leading. People it had formerly interested and amused him to watch, changed to puppets whose oddities shocked him; he began to exaggerate their absurdities and they appeared to his eyes as caricatures out of Sem's wittily sarcastic albums. Now he only watched absently their movements as a bored onlooker who yawns from his box at a play he has already seen. He knew by heart all their tricks and mannerisms.

In the middle of this moral crisis, he got a chance to go to China. Without a moment's hesitation, he accepted. The Far East attracted him; he wanted to see for himself what truth there was in all the queer novels which vaunted the joys of living so far away from old Europe, comparing, in high flown language, the superiority of the art, the beauty of the landscapes, with the ugliness of our civilisation.

Life in Peking fascinated him immediately. The brilliant light lending a gay and picturesque atmosphere to the most commonplace sight and making the least attractive ruin quite poetic, had strongly impressed his artistic nature. He never tired of looking at the city when it was bathed in the sunlight; even the tawdriness of the processions in the streets appealed to him; the sun rays playing on the yellow tiles of the Forbidden City always surprised him afresh. He loved to wander down the wide avenues or the Hutungs in the Chinese City thinking of their constancy since the time Marco Polo wandered there too.

He had not yet ceased to thrill as he passed through the lanes in the cypress wood near the Temple of Heaven and each time his fancy took him to his favourite spot, he recalled with pleasure, in the ruined loneliness of this holy place, the pomp of the ceremonies and the display of splendour in the time of the great Emperors.

The free and easy life here pleased him too. But something was worrying him just now. He could not define what it was. The remembrance of that scene on the Wall with Mrs. Brixton was hateful to him. The woman seemed to haunt him in some way. She had awakened strange emotions in his breast, aroused desires he had thought vanished since his arrival in the Far East, for he had forgotten his former adventures. Since coming to Peking he had had no sentimental adventures as yet, even if he had not been precisely chaste.

The discovery of his ardent desire for her astonished him. He found himself ready to do the most foolish things in order to possess her. But at the same time a vague feeling of disquietude seized him. He recalled the familiar landscapes of former times, not that he regretted that life but the urge to rid himself of these surroundings was upon him. He felt the atmosphere, full of the dust of ages, enclosed him like a shroud, dulled his energy and paralysed his will. Little by little his whole being was becoming impregnated with it like poison that slowly but surely does its deadly work of destruction.

All these thoughts passed through his mind; he did not notice the flight of time. Chu, the fat first "boy" appeared in the doorway, his broad face wearing its usual grin. In his pidgin English, he said "Missy come."

Downstairs Miss de Frissonges was getting out of her rickshaw. "How silly of me to be so late," she held out her hand to Jean, "nearly half an hour. Forgive me, but, as I was starting, the mail came. There were letters from France. I could not resist reading them at once. I do so love hearing the news from over there," she added suddenly thoughtful.

The *mafoos* brought up the ponies, two pretty Mongolian animals well kept, bright coated and rather small. Their shape and size recalled but little of their prototypes in Europe. Strong necked, too short bodies, a sportsman like Graziolli would criticize them, for he spouted pedigree on every occasion and boasted of the superiority of the thoroughbred or the anglo-arab.

However, these two ponies were not bad specimens of the strong little sure-footed animals who could do a dozen miles across country without a rest, jumping without any hesitation the *Kaoliang* hedges or the mud walls on the Chinese country side.

Used to all kinds of sports, the young girl mounted her pony without any help from Jean. She had scarcely touched the saddle when the pony became impatient and bounded forward. Shortening her reins she immediately controlled it, talking to it and stroking it gently. After a few attempts

at getting away, the animal calmed down and obeyed her without making any more difficulties. Maugrais could not help admiring the ease with which the girl mastered her mount, though for a moment he felt slightly anxious. Melle de Frissonges was slender and straightly built, and even the grey bowler, the usual hat for this sport, which is so unbecoming to most women, seemed to suit her. She had drawn her hair back under it and looked like a young boy; the exercise had caused the blood to rush to her face; and she was quite rosy as she listened to her companion's compliments. "Bravo, little lady," he said "you have an excellent seat and good hands."

"I can't take credit for that," she retorted. I have ridden since I was nine and at the Korean mines where I was born and where I lived until we came here it was almost my only distraction."

"Which way shall we go?" he asked as they left the Compound going down Legation Street. "Into the country, to the East or to the Race Course?"

"Not to the Race Course, heaps of people are there to-day."

She was going to say "Mrs. Brixton too," but some instinct warned her, so to hide her thoughts she added jokingly, "thanks, I have had enough of bores."

"All right, let's go to the Tomb of the Princess. We will follow the Canal and pretend we find it cool."

They turned to the left and soon reached the Hatamen Gate. Here they slowed up, for between the two gates where the Peking-Mukden line runs, a crowd of conveyances pressed in all directions.

Rickshaws with fat men stretched out sanctimoniously in them or with women clad in silks varying in shade from white to water green or pale blue, jostled against heavy carts with uneven teams of mules, horses and donkeys harnessed to them. They transported enormous pot-bellied jars of rice wine to the near-by market. A string of donkeys were scarcely visible under the loads of hay they carried, only their long ears could be seen. A few camels, not yet returned to their Mongolian pasture lands, surpassed in height all other animals. They were waiting, very patient and resigned, to cross the line. A few tufts of hair on their elongated scraggy necks were all that remained of their winter coat.

Pedestrians walked with caution, picking their way; some carried their purchases, tiny parcels hanging from a string, others carried a cage in which strutted the family bird. It was carefully protected from the hot sun by a blue linen cover.

In the midst of this crowd, a blind man, guided by some charitable person, struck a gong at intervals to warn people of his approach, so that they should make way for him or help him pass. In the midst of shouts and oaths, the wheelbarrows of some water carriers squeaked as they jolted over the uneven stones. Two cheery looking policemen were very deliberately trying to assist all that impatient mob. Suddenly, however, they got excited and shouted to make way for a travelling chair. Two richly caparaisoned mules were harnessed to it, one in front and the other behind. The animals ambling along swung the chair slowly and gently to and fro; the silken curtains were drawn aside to admit the air. Stretched on bright coloured, embroidered cushions, an old man in military uniform dozed. Some soldiers followed the chair. In all probability, some city official summoned to the capital.

Busy steering their mounts through this seething mass of humanity which would not stir in spite of the mafoo's cries, Jean and his companion did not speak. He felt good humoured now, he had forgotten his previous gloomy thoughts. He had ceased any attempt at self examination. The girl engrossed all his attention. He felt affection for her because he was convinced she was unlike other girls. She possessed great personality, quite different from the little girls in the Far East, from Shanghai or elsewhere who appeared from time to time at the Saturday evening dances at the Wagons Lits Hotel, and whom one ran across again sometimes at picnics. With them, he had only been able to broach a conversation so banal that he was always bored to tears; a game of tennis, a foxtrot was unmixed joy to them and their imagination could not soar beyond. They never thought there was anything else, any higher emotions than the satisfaction a cup of tea and cakes after some violent exercise procured them and which was their idea of a good time.

He felt incapable of sharing their simple enjoyment in life which needs a perfect physical balance but which also rather shows that those who possess it have their heart or brain in their stomachs. So up to now he had persistently avoided girls, preferring the society of women. He relied on them for more deeper impressions, for less worn sentiments and for a more complicated understanding of life's contingencies.

The pair were now out of the crowd; the ponies were restless at being made to wait among all the rickshaws; the young people gave them their heads and they galloped off. In a few strides they had crossed the willow bordered road leading to the gate at the east of the second wall that surrounds the Chinese City. The Mafoo followed, almost hidden in a cloud of dust.

On the right bank of the stream, the dyers were spreading out large pieces of stuff to dry; on the opposite side, weavers spun rapidly between two boards the brass ball fastened to each thread. They had fixed their skeins of silk on to trestles to obtain a stronger twist. A flock of geese and ducks were feeding, white specks on the dark water.

"I did not see you at the American Legation ball the other night," said Maugrais, as they slowed up. They pulled into a walk as they went over the old stone bridge thrown across the Peking-Tientsin Canal. After the siege of the Legations by the Boxers in 1900, when the railway was cut, the first people to leave passed this way.

"No," she answered, "I went to Pa Ta Chu for the week end with Mme. de Beaurelois. Didn't you know she had been in the Hills for some time. They have rented the big temple at the top for two months and every Saturday regularly they go there. I preferred accepting their invitation to dancing. We went on horseback; by Pa Li Tchoang it doesn't take more than an hour and a half."

"Were you many?"

"No, we three, your friend Chatours and young Graziolli who was invited by Mme. de Beaurelois for me, Mme. de Maricourt without her husband and the British officer who is beginning a flirtation with her. You see," she added smiling, "flirtations were not ignored in the programme and our hostess had forgotten nothing."

"I hope you enjoyed yourself."

"Yes, pretty well. All day Sunday we went for long walks; we visited the Temple where the mummy of Kang Hsi's father lies. You know whom I mean; that Emperor who, tired of the splendours of this world, did like Charles Quint, he withdrew into a monastery and spent the rest of his life praying for forgiveness of his sins. After dinner, we were not fatigued enough to sleep, so we strolled about under the great trees on a kind of esplanade overlooking the entire plain."

"Graziolli's chatter annoyed me. He understood at last and went to join the others grouped round Mme. de Beaurelois. They left me to myself; I sat on a stone wall and dreamed, dozing. Not a sound rose from the slumbering earth. Only the bell of a mule, as his shoes struck the stony road, broke the silence of the night from time to time. Far away in the pale moonlight, the silver face of the lake in the Summer palace could be distinguished. The farm dogs in the neighbourhood barked occasionally, answering each other; in the valley below, the lights went out one by one. Only a reddish glow marked the great city, and a dark blurred outline, its walls."

"For one moment I thought I was in some corner of the Alps. I was living in a large house, half farm, half mansion.

As if ashamed of the crevices, its walls were covered with ivy and honeysuckle. The harvest was in, it was the end of a warm summer's day; the last cart, full of golden wheat was slowly wending its way home drawn by two pairs of white oxen, their horns decorated with ribbons. The harvest chief having climbed to the top, seemed to preside over this festivity. He held a branch of a birch tree in one hand and a bunch of cornflowers in the other. The youths, their faces tanned by the sun, followed slowly, their coats over their arms, their shirts open. They had forgotten the day's fatigue; one was singing a song in broad dialect, whilst the others joined in the chorus. The girls from the farms, with poppies in their hair, followed the procession. A little later they paired off in front of the house and danced to the sounds of fife and drum. I was expected to open the dance with the harvest chief and then to dance with each man in turn. I had reached this part of my delightful dream when Graziolli brutally broke the spell by some silly remark about the coming tennis tournament in which I am playing with him."

"Well," said Jean, "if that is your only reason for being annoyed with him, it isn't serious and your flirtation is not compromised," he added, smiling, for he liked to tease her.

They had now left the town. In the green country, the kaoliang fields lay side by side with plantations of maize and soya bean. Here and there coolies worked, a large straw covering protecting their heads. The brown skins of the naked children running about the lanes made them look like little bronze men. The cicadas were singing at the top of their shrill voices celebrating the splendour of the Chinese summer. Above their song one could hear the sharp noise of the click of the wooden wheels a little donkey was turning patiently to draw up the water used for irrigating the fields.

In the villages, the Chinese women gossiped from their doorstep, or else, walking painfully on their tiny bound feet, slowly worked the mill used to ground the millet, its golden dust filling the air. The sun shed a strong light on the surroundings, it brought out the thousand and one shades of green, clothing the country.

Like the warm breath of nature in labour, the scent of the earth rose from the ground.

The open air had put a colour into the girl's cheeks, her golden curls escaped from under her hat; the joy of being alive shone in her eyes, the look of weariness and boredom had completely disappeared. Jean began to realize he liked to be with her; he had rid himself of the vision of the American, even though, only a short while ago, she had filled his every thought. There was too great a contrast between Melle de Frissonges and that diabolical woman whose blue grey eyes sometimes looked like steel. He knew her strange beauty attracted and fascinated him, but he feared her all the same. This girl whom until now he had simply found a little less commonplace than the others, appeared to have a fresh and charming nature and her naive outbursts interested him. She was like a barely unclosed, delicately perfumed, tender flower in the midst of those plants whose acrid scent went to one's head.

His growing passion for Mrs. Brixton rose and fell as a fever. At times it was more acute, but when the attack was finished, he sought, like an invalid, a little freshness. The sight of this simple and pure girl slaked his thirst for awhile and snatched him from the burning dreams by which he was obsessed.

They reached the spot where the canal narrows, to give more force to the water that turns the mills, before falling with the noise of a waterfall into its bed lower down. A wooden bridge joins the two banks on which a few inns are huddled. Seated before cups of scalding tea or sharing flat maize cakes, the boatmen lazed under the arches, smoking their long small-bowled pipes. On the bank carved in the stone, two large dragons, like water genii, seemed to guard this picturesque spot.

"Don't you think this view is delightful," said Jean, "It is much prettier than the work of any of the Dutch masters. You must own that on a beautiful day like today, you are glad to be in China where the sun is so lavish of his light. I am sure you don't regret the stream and the little mill you mentioned to me on the Wall the other day."

"Of course not," she said smiling, "but I am not in the same frame of mind. On the contrary, I feel I shall certainly regret this old country of China, I have so often hated. For I have not told you the great news, I am soon going back to France."

"Oh, you are thinking of leaving us."

"Yes, Papa has declared he wants to try and interest the banks in his affairs. He means to form a company for his mine. He says he begins to feel he is growing old, he has made enough money to live comfortably in some corner of the provinces. He will grow roses, translate Horace just like a retired cavalry officer, play bridge with his neighbours, and ... busy himself with finding me a husband. And you, Mr. Maugrais aren't you also thinking of going home for good? How long have you been here?"

"Nearly six years, Melle de Frissonges, I am already looked upon as an old resident. I am pointed out to the new arrivals as one who knew the splendours of the

old regime, the carrying chair, the pigtails, the hats with peacock feathers and Sir Robert Hart's green tie. My opinion is asked when any one wants to buy a *Ming* vase or a *Kosseu*; I am steward of the race course and a heeded member of several other committees. In short, my word carries weight," he added laughing, "So you see I linger here." Then becoming serious, he went on, "Certainly I get homesick sometimes for Europe, but could I return and throw myself again into the vortex of Paris? Each day I see my pals go; I often envy them but I haven't the strength of mind to wrench myself away from the easy nonchalant life into which I feel myself gradually sinking. Yes, sometimes I feel like a man who has gone too far, drawn by a deceptive mirage and who finds himself in the quicksands. Every movement he makes sucks him down deeper; soon he loses his footing; his cries are stifled in his throat as it closes; he can no longer call for help, so conquered, he resigns himself and does not even make gestures he knows are useless."

"What ideas," said the girl; "I don't recognize you like that. I thought you were skeptical and blasé, but I find you fatalist, resigned and defenceless. You must react. Besides, how do you know that no kind soul will pass by your quicksands and hold you out a helping hand?"

She had spoken without thinking. He looked at her; she coloured a little.

"Our ride will end in a walk," she said, "Shall we trot?"

She gathered up her reins, the pony quickened his pace and Jean's followed. The path was broad enough to ride abreast so the dust did not bother them. After a few strides the ponies broke into a gallop; the flies had been worrying them, their legs needed stretching. In a few minutes they were in sight of the tomb, a wood marked the spot. Some urchins, hoping for a tip, offered to hold the ponies and ran along behind them.

A shrivelled-up old guardian, warned by one of the children, arrived, limping, on the scene, a bunch of keys in his hand, just as the two young people were dismounting. A blind beggar wrapped in his rags lay on the ground, asleep, his wooden bowl beside him. At the sound of voices he woke and began to beg.

The ponies, their bridles removed by the mafoo, started to graze greedily on the grass covering the alley of statues that leads to the tomb.

"You have probably been here often," said Jean to the young girl, as they went slowly by the marble giants. In their venerable immobility they seemed like servants or familiar animals waiting a sign from their dead masters whose spirits hovered near.

"Don't you think the Chinese have a stronger sense of the respect due to those who are no longer with us? Their devotion to their dead is so great. Our narrow graveyards are just cemeteries where the dead are not even free to escape from those whom they were unable to avoid in this world. The whole of China, on the contrary, is one huge cemetery where rich and poor alike can rest in the midst of familiar landscapes. Death smiles here; a tomb is not a sad monument where only a short epitaph recalls him who sleeps his last sleep below."

"Look at the beauty of this tomb; this marble column, resting on the sacred tortoise, emblem of eternal happiness, is inscribed with long tirades, full of poetry, extolling the merits of the illustrious person who is buried here. During his lifetime, the walls of his yamen hid his home from curious eyes. Now a double wall jealously guards the funeral altar where his soul comes at nightfall, to partake of the offerings. These great ash trees, in the middle of the shrunken stumps in the plain, spread their shade over the *stupa* which marks the place where the coffin rests and the light breeze rustles through

SILHOUETTES OF PEKING

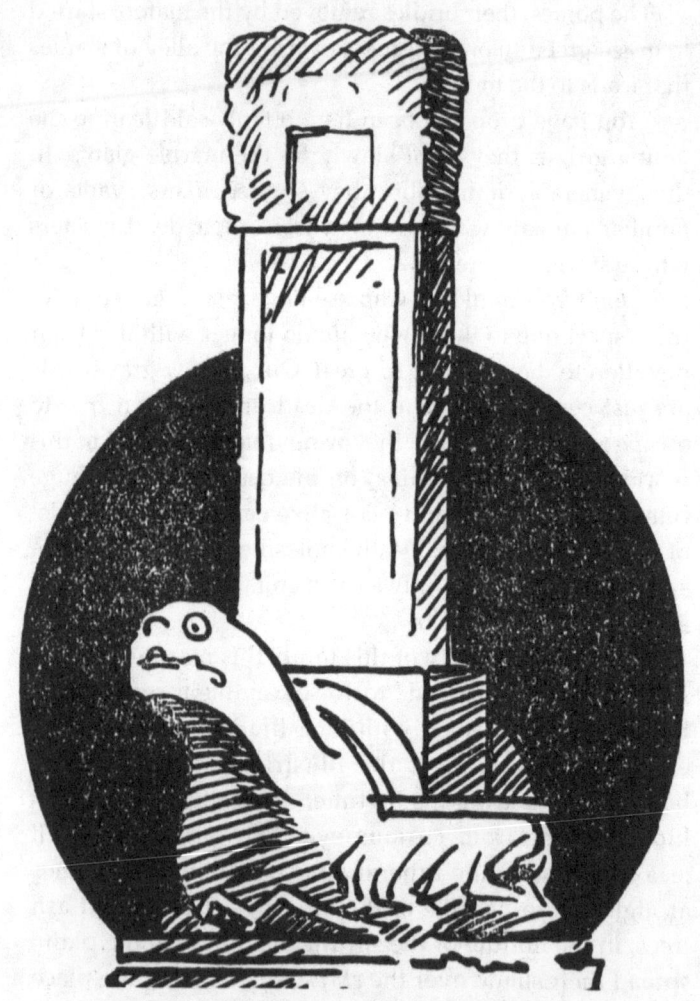

their finely veined leaves and he who lies in this tomb is lulled to sleep by their soft murmur."

"How poetical you are to-day, Mr. Maugrais," said little Melle de Frissonges laughing. "I don't believe you even know why this monument was erected. You probably believe the usual tale, that it was erected by a sorrowing husband to the memory of an Imperial princess, endowed with all the virtues. Well, that is not so, it is the tomb of one of the Emperor Ch'ien Lung's servants. He had amassed great riches and his all-powerful master, in a sudden impulse, raised this sumptuous habitation to him. The funeral inscription you mentioned just now is a proof. I know, one of the Russian Legation Interpreters translated it for me last spring."

"Your knowledge puts me in an embarrasing position. You are quite right, my soul is too poetic, and as you wish to arrest the flight of my imagination, I must confess the offerings I spoke of just now are probably the remains of a pic nic: look at the greasy paper lying about everywhere. As for the pious visitors who come to decorate the altar, they are doubtless some of the people from the different Legation guards, judging from the signatures on the walls."

They roamed about joking, when suddenly the sky became overcast; dark clouds passed over the hill tops.

"We had better go home," said Maugrais. "If we loiter too long, we shall be overtaken by the shower." The mafoo was already holding the ponies for them; they hastened to mount. Jean proposed cutting across country to save time. They could no longer ride abreast; she took the lead. The sky, so clear in the early afternoon, had clouded over, the atmosphere had become oppressive. The threatened storm came nearer; the pair galloped on in silence.

Maugrais felt himself influenced by the sadness which covered the landscape, so bright and gay a little while ago under the hot caresses of the sun. Like a mantle of lead the shadows fell across the country side, the green fields quivered as if the earth were shaking with fear; the reeds near the bank moaned plaintively.

He turned over in his mind the conversation of a while ago; he recalled the sinking into the quicksands, gradually they had risen all round him. When finally he realized his danger and wished to escape it was already too late, the efforts he made were of no avail and only increased his anguish. He resigned himself to his fate and ended in a slow agony.

He had already tarried here a long time, gradually the memory of the friends he had left in France was getting blurred by the distance; letters were becoming scarcer; one after the other the links that bound him to the old world were breaking, his scattered family diminished almost daily. When he left France, his mother had just died; last year his father followed her into the tomb. He saw himself growing older here in the midst of always fresh faces; other people only passed through, he alone seemed to tarry. A day would arrive when he, too, would return to France, but sick at heart; it would be too late, he would find no friendly faces; over there, as here, he would be alone in the midst of unknown people, seeking shelter in a embittered selfishness which would only increase the void round him.

As for this American, he wanted her passionately with his whole being; an unconquerable force drew him to her;

he was fascinated. Fate meant him to become her prey, but nevertheless, the helping hand so sorely needed to prevent his sinking deeper was, it seemed, close by. He had, he was almost certain, only to make a movement to grasp it and the horrible nightmare that pursued him and against which he was struggling would vanish.

The young couple had now reached a turning; the ponies rather blown, had slowed down. Jean's suddenly shied, a crow rose slowly into the air, croaking. A dark heap lay in a field bordering the road. It was a coffin, recently deposited there until the grave should be dug. On the road, some figures were moving away; the family of the dead were going home. The procession could scarcely have been imposing, only five or six relatives, in their long white mourning robes, accompanied the dead to his last resting place. They stood aside to allow the ponies to pass. A few paces further on, the bearers were scattered along the road, their long red poles on their shoulders. The coolies followed with the beggars hired for the occasion, bringing back the various things which figure as a matter of course in the funeral procession of all Chinese, even those of the lowest classes. Draped in green smocks with conventional design, their heads covered with a piece of filthy felt, decorated with cock feathers dyed red and slightly moth eaten, they walked along. One man carried a wicker basket containing the white chicken which, a few minutes ago, had been placed at the head of the coffin. By its presence, it had forced the soul of the dead to accompany, as far as the burying place, the body it was tempted to abandon.

They also met the red-clad musicians, carrying on their backs the now useless cymbals with which they had beaten

SILHOUETTES OF PEKING

time for the march of the procession. A child had taken, from the hands of a bearer, the funeral horn with wide flag, whose sad melope sounded alternatively with the clang of the gongs, beaten to keep the evil spirits away. As Jean and his companion passed the child blew a harsh blast, prolonged like a sob into a plaintive moan.

Jean, buried in his sad thoughts, suddenly shivered. Large drops of rain were falling, making dark spots in the dust on the ground.

"We must hurry," he said urging on his pony, and they galloped in silence to the city gates.

CHAPTER VI

THERE was bridge that day from 5 o'clock, at Mme. de Maricourt's. She had met Jean on the Wall in the morning, and, though he was neither an enthusiastic nor a brilliant bridge player, he had promised her to come. If he did not play, he could always talk. Chatours and the Argentine Minister would be there; the two Beaurelois, the little de Frissonges girl, Mrs. Brixton, in short every one whom the heat had not yet driven from Peking to Pei Ta Ho or Shan Hai Kwan.

He had allowed himself to be persuaded and now his rickshaw was taking him towards the Hutung in the Chinese City where the young people had taken a house. They lived in an old yamen which used to belong to

Prince Su and which they had arranged with a great deal of taste.

Before the brilliant-hued door, a few carriages waited. Among them Jean at once recognized Mrs. Brixton's. Her men servants wore scarlet coats.

The *Kai men ti*, venerable as he should be in a well-kept house, hastened to greet the young man and to shew him the way in.

They had first to cross a courtyard, passing through one of those round openings pierced through a brick wall, so characteristic of Chinese architecture. The gnarled trunk of a century-old wisteria grew against the wall; although so late in the season the tree was still covered with bunches of mauve flowers. The second courtyard was protected from the sun by a *pang*, a kind of scaffolding on which are placed coarsely woven straw mats. It was almost shady underneath, the temperature perceptibly less than outside. To the left and right, in large polished earthen-ware jars the traditional gold fish, goggled eyed, lolled on the water.

The drawing room doors stood wide open.

"How nice of you to keep your promise, Mr. Maugrais," said Mme. de Maricourt affectedly as Jean entered. She was alone, seated at a small table set for tea. She was scolding the servant for forgetting some plates of cakes.

"You see, I am abandoned, the men and Mrs. Brixton have already started their game over there on the verandah. My husband will give up his place to you bye and bye, but first sit down for a minute and flirt with me."

"I shall love too. Besides, I play badly and I prefer disparaging my friends gracefully with you, rather than making a grand slam in a no trump hand."

"All right, then I shall have no scruples about keeping you with me. But you know gossiping is not my strong point and I never talk scandal."

"How surprising. I did not know that any woman in this little village of Peking could live without following the usual custom. I am sure you are like all the rest and sometimes succumb to temptation."

"Well, perhaps; I don't want to make myself out better than I am. I'll tell you what people are saying about you."

"What have they confided to you? That I am peculiar blasé and something of a man hater and that I am partial to paradoxes?"

"Not at all, you are right off the scent. I was told you have lately been very attentive to the little de Frissonges girl. It appears you go for long sentimental rides with her."

"People are idiots," retorted Maugrais sharply. "Of course I find her very nice and I like her quite well, but what else will they invent?"

"There, there, calm yourself, otherwise I shall think there is some truth in the talk," she added laughing. "But after all, it would not be such a bad thing. As for me, I adore the child and I am sure she would make you a charming wife in spite of the rather independent airs she gives herself."

"Oh I see what is matter. You have been attacked by the matrimonial fever. Take care," he said jokingly, "it is very dangerous in this climate. Unfortunately, you are out of luck with me, because confidence for confidence, whenever a woman appeals to me, I discover she is already provided with a husband."

She burst out laughing. "Do you say that for me?"

"Perhaps, who knows?"

Footsteps sounded outside. Chatours, the Beaurelois couple and Melle de Frissonges arrived all together.

'What a pity," said Maugrais dryly, "I was just going to make you a declaration."

Mme. de Maricourt hastened to offer tea and iced drinks. The usual banalities exchanged, they talked of the Brazilian Minister's sale. It had taken place the day before yesterday. Chatours announced he had been there; he had been told there would be some porcelain and some brocades.

"Did you buy anything?" asked Mme. de Beaurelois.

"No, the so-called rare pieces were all more or less chipped vases. On the other hand, there were a quantity of old top hats which sold like hot cakes. They are very popular since the advent of the Republic."

"What, do you mean he also put his old clothes up for sale?"

"Of course, he turned everything he could into money. Ask Graziolli," he said turning to the young man who had just come in.

"Certainly," he affirmed, "there were even some rather worn drawers belonging to the Ministress; I bought them. Lined with rose coloured silk they will make lovely lamp shades. What are you laughing at? I am not joking; besides it will complete my collection. My dining room comes from the French legation, a departing secretary sold it to me; my bed used to belong to one of the Customs people and my drawing room furniture was the property of the last Russian military attaché. Oh, I nearly forgot the most important thing; I bought my bath and heater from the last director but one of the Sino Bulgarian Bank."

"For my part," said Beaurelois, "I never go to sales; they disgust me a bit. When I leave, I shall try and sell to my friends whatever I don't take with me. But I will certainly not have my house overrun by every body who chooses to come in. The Chinese dealers in old clothes are only too glad to see the inside of a European's house. They make themselves quite at home there, ensconcing themselves in the arm chairs; in reality they make fun of us behind our backs and snap their fingers at us."

"Anyhow, my dear," Maugrais said, "Whatever they buy always finds its way eventually into the houses in the Diplomatic Quarter. A play was running in Paris some years ago called 'The Torch,' the author showed that the torch of science went from hand to hand. Here we are less ambitious, only the furniture passes from hand to hand. When we call upon newcomers for the first time, we are sure to find friends; a small familiar table, a sofa with a history and which could tell tales if it were not as discreet as a diplomat."

The women smiled; Mme. de Beaurelois looked thoughtful, her eyes half closed. She seemed to be absent from the people surrounding her. Chatours watched her amusedly from the corner of his eye. He guessed her thoughts; she could plainly see her beautiful divan, with its comfortable yellow silk cushions, sold at auction when she had left Peking and she was recalling distinct memories of some ex-conjugal embraces to which she had abandoned herself with joy in the days of temptation, giving herself without stint, and fulfilling without reserve, her role of the great lover.

"Is it true you are going away?" asked Mme. de Maricourt turning to the de Frissonges girl.

"Yes, my father wishes to go and live in France. But I do not think we shall leave just yet. We shall wait for the end of the summer."

"Then the series of farewell dinners will not begin at once. I am sure you must be charmed with the idea of becoming better acquainted with the joys of Europe. Aren't you delighted at the thought?"

"Yes, of course. I wanted so much to go and live there that now I am a little afraid of finding myself out of my

element. Besides, I hate to think of leaving for ever the country where I was born and where I have spent my childhood. Shall I be happy in France? I thought so, but now I am not certain. I shall tumble into the midst of strangers, I shall be friendless. You know the oft repeated saying *Partir c'est mourir un peu*. Well, I feel I shall leave a little of myself behind me and it makes me sad."

"Oh," said Graziolli, "you'll soon get used to it. Besides, as soon as you land you will be swamped with invitations.

Remember you will learn all the fashionable dances at least two years before we do. And if you leave at the beginning of autumn, you will be in France for the big tennis matches. You will see the Peking Club tournament is only child's play in comparison."

The girl did not answer. She was lost in thought and these remarks left her cold.

Some one started to talk about curios, asking to see Maricourt's new purchase. He was a rabid collector of snuff bottles in all colours and shapes.

"Is it true he bought a beautiful one recently, a little jade snuff bottle in a wonderful shade of green?"

Like every one else, Mme. de Maricourt had caught the curio-collecting mania. No one escapes in Peking. Once or twice a week, she and her husband went the rounds of the shops, peering into every corner and hoping to put their hand on *the* rare piece. She took her guests at once to the room to shew them the snuff bottle. It occupied the place of honour in a cabinet against the wall. The shelves were crowded with snuff bottles in battle array.

The Argentina Minister, expert in hard stone, went into ecstasies; he took up the jade piece very carefully and held it to the light. It was a very dark green, almost giving the illusion of an emerald; the carving was particularly beautiful. All the upper surface had been worked and was carved in garlands of flowers. The tracery seemed to enclose the entire rounded part of the bottle.

Don Luis de Cordobas declared it to be the most beautiful thing of its kind he had ever seen. He was sure it had taken at least a year to carve and was certainly very old, for it was smooth to the touch and the polish of the old pieces is impossible to imitate.

"You probably know how jade is carved," he said. "I was curious enough to enter a shop in one of the small streets on Chien Men once where the jade carvers have their workshops. First the piece of jade is shaped by experts like those employed by our own sculptors. Circular saws worked by pedals are used for this part. Then the artist begins; the stone is worn down patiently by means of a grindstone on which is scattered slightly damped jade powder or else it is cut with a diamond as is glass. Finally the polishing begins. This is obtained by rubbing first on ordinary polishing stone and then on emery. Most of the jade comes from Eastern Turkestan; it is taken from the Khotan and Yarkand mountains or else picked up in the shape of worn pebbles in the beds of the rivers that come down from these mountains. There is also some jade found in the Yunnan and in Burma."

Jean had not followed the others; he stayed where he was, thinking of the de Frissonges girl. Her words had struck him; her sad look had moved him and he wanted to talk to her, to learn her real thoughts and to try and console her.

When Graziolli had alluded to the pleasures awaiting her in Europe, he had noticed a look of pain flit over her face. From the bottom of his heart he had cursed the tactless young man whose thoughts were turned only to dancing and sport and for whom life consisted solely of a ball room or a tennis court.

"What a fool," he thought.

"What is the matter," he asked approaching the girl. "You must chase away these blue devils," and as she did

SILHOUETTES OF PEKING

not reply, he added "You are on the point of obtaining your heart's desire. You have no reason for being unhappy; I don't see any great happiness for you like Graziolli does, but what I do see is, pretty as you are, you will soon find a nice husband."

"Oh," she said, "I am not thinking of getting married yet."

"But you should. I don't see you becoming an old maid. Besides marriage is the natural finish to a girls' education. Although I am not Mme. de Thebes or any other clairvoyant, I can easily foretell you will end up by being tranquilly happy, adoring your husband. You will make a good mother who will bring up the children beautifully."

She smiled, "Mr. Maugrais, you are horrid; you are making fun of me. All that sounds attractive, but it is just a dream. I may only meet with disillusions and bitterness over there. You see, what I regret the most in leaving China are the very few real friends in whom I can confide, who understand me when I tell them my troubles. I am afraid when I am in Europe, I shall not find any one in whom to confide, I shall have to keep my thoughts to myself. At least here," she added in an undertone, "I can always ask your advice. You are not like all the others and you seem to like me."

She had said all this in one breath. She stopped, a little embarrassed, fearing she had betrayed herself, that she shown too clearly the young man attracted her and that her greatest regret in going away was having to leave Jean. She was not yet quite sure whether she loved him, but gradually she was getting accustomed to being glad to see him. When he talked to her, she was always content. After dinners, when groups formed themselves in drawing rooms, she nearly always found herself in a corner with him. These little private conversations lengthened out either because the pair lingered, chattering, or else because the other people, with unconscious complicity, left them to themselves.

However, Jean had often been removed from her side by Mrs. Brixton, who had interrupted them. This strangely beautiful woman, whose lithe body moved felinely and whose sometimes tender and imploring eyes occasionally darted piercing, eagle-like glances at him, inspired her with feelings of fear and even terror. The girl felt here was the enemy. Some instinct warned her this woman would make her suffer; she was defenceless and she wanted to cry out: "I have never done you any harm, please spare me. You are beautiful, you are greatly admired. Leave me alone, I am only a weakling, without weapons to fight you. Don't take my one friend from me; he is the only person who pities me and in whom I can confide."

The bridge game was finished; Mrs. Brixton declared she did not want to play any longer. She went towards the other room with Maricourt who looked for a fresh partner.

"Well dear lady, and how was the game?" asked the Argentina Minister.

"Don't talk to me about it, I was the only loser."

Don Luis de Cordobas smiled enigmatically. You know the saying unlucky at cards, lucky in love."

The American, a little uneasy, did not reply. She feared this strange man; he had the reputation of being a woman hater, and she had tried her powers of fascination on him in vain. Was he laughing at her? Had he guessed her fancy for Maugrais? Did he know anything about the insult on the Wall? Her woman's pride had been humiliated by it, but it had also seemed to change her fancy into passion so that, first humble and imploring, then scornful and proud, she wanted both to give herself and to deny herself to the man who had repulsed her.

She did not speak for a minute, but turned her head away. She caught sight of Mlle de Frissonges sitting next to Jean. Suddenly, a wish to hurt this girl seized her, this chit for whom Maugrais showed a partiality.

"So you are still in Peking," she said. Then with a touch of sarcasm in her voice. "Oh of course, I have forgotten, my husband told me he had seen you riding the other day with Mr. Maugrais."

"Yes, Mrs. Brixton, we went to the Princess Tomb."

"It is a charming place to dream in, especially for just two people," said the American spitefully. "You are lucky to find men willing in spite of the heat, to go for sentimental rides with you." Then she broke off and listened absently to what was being said around her. A few minutes later she rose and passing near Maugrais, said, looking straight into his eyes: "Will you see me home, I must go now."

Just now when she had mentioned the ride, Jean had felt humbled by the scornful tone in which she had spoken to the girl; but ashamed like a school boy found out, he had not dare to speak. Now he reproached himself for his cowardice. This woman's glance disturbed him although it attracted him like a magnet; he obeyed and stammering a few vague excuses he followed the American.

As she watched him go, a pang of anguish shot through the girl. Unconsciously her hand clenched on the card case she carried; a look of intense pain contorted her delicate features. Suddenly she felt like bursting into tears. But she made an effort to control herself and she was able to answer quite naturally some ordinary question Graziolli put to her.

When the American and Maugrais appeared, the carriage drew up at the door. Mrs. Brixton hesitated. "It is cooler now," she said, "shall we walk a little; I have not had my usual walk on the Wall to-day. Come along, a little turn on foot will do us good."

Maugrais agreed and she sent the carriage away.

They went down the street in silence. He had obeyed like a machine just now and he still felt as if his head was empty; he could not collect his ideas, he was absolutely powerless, submitting to this woman's influence. A mere glance from her was enough to magnetise him.

Slim in her well cut white serge dress, Mrs. Brixton looked very young, her figure remained lithe and supple giving her the air of a woman of 25, whose lengthy stay in the Far East had hastened her development. Under her coat, her silk open necked blouse left exposed her milk white throat. Her soft skin seemed to beg caresses and under the thin material her flesh still looked firm and appetising.

A large black ribboned Manila straw hat gave an appearance of slenderness to her features which had not yet coarsened. Her short white skirt exposed her shapely legs ending in slight ankles and well proportioned high instepped feet. She wore well fitting buckskin shoes.

Jean was the first to speak.

"You were a little unkind just now to Melle de Frissonges," he said. "You know how sensitive she is. Under her free and easy ways she hides a delicate nature. She must be treated gently. I am sure you hurt her feelings, she curled up like the sensitive plant she is."

"Oh, you seem to be intimately acquainted with her. You must have studied psychology during your rides with her. I think you are growing naive, you, the blasé rake. A little girl makes you her confidant and that is sufficient to influence you like a school boy just out of college Take care, Mr. Maugrais, you will be getting ridiculous."

"What are you insinuating?"

"My goodness, it is easy to see you are falling in love. That goose, that sham-pure girl will end by leading you straight to the altar. I always thought you required something young, but beware . . . You are slightly the worse for wear. I wonder if you won't have some difficulty in fulfilling your conjugal duties. Believe me, my dear, you will make a fool of yourself." Jean did not reply immediately. He could feel he was growing cowardly and he was ashamed; he wanted to make excuses and to tell her she was inventing.

"Never," he asserted. "I would not do such an idiotic thing. I assure you it never even entered my head." Then with an attempt at joking, he added, "Do you see me as the father of a family and jumping the kids on my knee. No, no, I am not cut out for that sort of thing. What makes you think I am, you who know me so well. The girl is nothing to me, as you know. She aroused my interest because she is a little different from the others, that's all. I am too ripe for anything so green." Then without pausing he went on, "Do you realize how truly charming you look in that white dress, it suits you down to the ground."

"I am glad I meet with your approval," she answered.

He continued, "Just now, when you asked me to see you home, every thing else went out of my head; I followed you without even stopping to say good-bye to any one. You attract me as the light attracts a moth. You have bewitched me, I no longer have any will of my own, your very glance holds me fascinated."

He spoke in a dull, hurried tone. Her eyes, as she turned them to him were almost tender but a second after, an angry light flashed in them and with a disdainful curl of her lip, she answered: "Your declaration, if it is really one, is a little late, Mr. Maugrais. But I understand your situation. *Entre les deux votre coeur* balance, as you say in French. But you probably don't know my motto."

"No, tell me what it is, perhaps it is all or nothing. It would really lack originality if it was."

At first she remained silent, absorbed in her thoughts. Then suddenly standing quite still, she slowly uttered the verses from Goethe's Erlkonig.

"Und bist du nicht willing so brauch ich Gewalt."

Maugrais cast a glance at her, that instant he received the impression she was made of steel.

"Gewalt," he said, "Force..."

She gave a laugh in which veiled threats and good humour mingled.

"Not physical force, naturally... I leave that to Immersteht."

They had reached the bridge connecting the Glacis with the Legation Quarter. A sentry, perched on the wall, watched them smiling to himself. They passed under the acacia trees along the British Legation avenue and walked on silently for a few seconds.

The American suddenly slackened her pace, she touched Maugrais' hand lightly and said as if to herself:

"Jean, Jean, sometimes I think you must be blind or else what is still worse, just banal. I am afraid, my friend, you will hesitate too long between the insipidity of happiness and the dazzling joys of suffering and pain." She said no more. A rickshaw stopped before them. Mr. Brixton got out.

"Hullo, he said cheerily, shaking Jean's hand energetically. I haven't seen you for ages. Come in and have a whiskey and soda."

Rather upset at this encounter at such a moment, the young man refused.

"No thanks, I must go to the Club," he said mechanically.

He took his leave and vanished in the direction of Legation street.

CHAPTER VII

WHEN the long file of rickshaws, horsemen and pedestrians crowded out of the town by the Ping Tze Men and dispersed along the broad road leading to the Western Hills, the sun was yet high in the Heavens. But it seemed already weary of darting forth its rays during the long hours and was ready to descend slowly towards the panting earth. A small motor followed the long string, its horn hooting shrilly from time to time. The noise it made disturbed the philosophical camels and caused them to shy in a manner not at all seemly to their stately dignity. The people in the car alighted at the gates and, like a flight of doves, a cloud of white frocks scattered about the golden road. To avoid the dust, they went into the *kaoliang* fields which stretched as far as the eye could see. Here and there were clumps of trees throwing their shade over the solitary graves where proud and watchful stood great stone monsters.

The ponies climbed the bank; in the radiant sunlight, their riders looked like equestrian statues surveying the brilliant country side. Only the rickshaws were unable to leave the road; they advanced slowly, their wheels sunk in the ruts and hidden in a cloud of dust. Gay voices sounded, calling to each other from group to group; fresh laughter rang from out the high *kaoliang*, such infectious laughter that even the horrible beggars who haunt the outskirts of the city stopped to look at the crowd of gay foreigners, the glimmer of a smile on their dull, worn faces.

"Is it much farther Wan Hei Lo?" Mme. de Beaurelois' soft voice was heard asking.

Lolling back in her rickshaw she already looked tired and seemed to beg a comforting answer. Her frock, which showed every curve of her body, was perfectly cut but a trifle too elegant for a picnic in the country. She was hidden under a flaming red parasol, a moving light to lead the excursionists.

"At least another half hour," replied Maugrais riding slowly along the edge of the road.

The Baroness pouted. "I am anxious to arrive. I am dying of thirst for this rickshaw jolts me up terribly."

Maugrais smiled at this; he appreciated at its just value the logic of women. He answered cheerily, "How I wish I might carry you in my arms, dear lady."

"Beware of trying to do that, for you would antagonize two people at the same time," retorted the Baroness, delighted to touch, even so lightly, on the subject of love.

Maugrais became serious again; he said nothing but pressed his pony who jumped a ditch.

At that moment two women rode up. They looked very smart and both were perfect horsewomen. They were Mrs. Brixton and Miss de Frissonges. Their ponies, one black and the other chestnut, were so close to each other that they almost seemed to touch; their two heads one fair and the other dark, were also very near together as if they were exchanging confidences.

Chatours, striding across country, raised great clouds of dust. As he went, he discussed with Dr. Borioni, the eminent Chinese scholar, the age of the marble tortoises who sleep overwhelmed by the weight of the commemorative columns hoisted on their backs.

Mrs. Immersteht, forced by her husband to go on horseback, a thing she hated, stuck to Brixton, and tried to prove she could be intelligent even on the back of a "fourteen hands." Graziolli, Vladowsky and Maxwell surrounded Mme. de Wolf's rickshaw, telling inconceivably scandalous stories to which she listened, impassive and unbending, like a queen on her throne. Count de Cordobas, in a rickshaw, his eyes closed, turned his face to the sun and his chilly little person seemed to delight in the warmth of the sun bath. Old de Frissonges and Beaurelois followed, quietly talking business as if they had moved their offices into these burning plains. And behind, all alone, his immense stature shewing up in the midst of the fields, Immersteht flourished his whip, urging on his horse and uttering vague exclamations that could only be addressed to the crumbling bricks of the graves or to the white tortoises, motionless in the sun.

"Here is Wan Hei Lo," exclaimed Chatours, who, having passed rickshaws and horsemen, appeared to be advancing to take possession of an enemy post.

"Look at those huge fir trees behind the walls, Wan Hei Lo is there, the mysterious country Palace of the Ming Emperors."

At a short distance away, to the West, in the midst of *kaoliang* fields, a little enclosure was visible. The old stones had acquired a rosy colour, the work of ages. A clump of trees peopled the spot; ancestral and dignified black firs, sad and resigned willows bending towards the dried bed of a canal. The gaps in the walls were smothered in wild vegetation, the outline of tumble-down pavilions shewed up the painted angles of their falling roofs, making a last effort to stand against the sky. Everything had that aspect of desolation, neglect and profound melancholy of survivors of past ages, which, amid the vain hideousness of our time, seems to continue mutely an ancient solitary and noble dream.

"Wan Hei Lo, Wan Hei Lo," repeated Chatours. The words sounded like soft Oriental music. "Ladies and gentlemen, before entering this sanctuary, look at it well, it sleeps in peace in the sunlight, lost in an ocean of *kaoliang*."

The rickshaws halted, the riders came up and the whole group stayed a moment in silent contemplation.

An old peasant passed, mounted on a small donkey. Seated almost on the tail of the intelligent animal — so unjustly flouted by man's stupidity — he had left the reins loose knowing full well the beast would pick its own way. His eyes roaming, he sang in a high soprano a Chinese song; its melancholy tune and magnetic rhythm seemed to call up from their graves white spectres, dripping with sweat and tears. He did not notice the gay company a few

paces from him. He passed almost touching them, without turning his head, as we often pass blindly by some great events and magnificent opportunities, feeling probably by some instinct that, before the unfathomable depths of our souls, they are puerile and worthless.

"Forward," shouted Immersteht, "I hope we don't mean to spend all night here. Follow me."

He urged his horse along the canal to a curious old bridge. The stone supports, breaking through the rotten planks, made it look like a toothless jaw. A squat, quadrangular turret, studded with loop-holes and pierced by a low door, guarded the entrance to the grounds. Leaving the ponies and rickshaws, they all entered Wan Hei Lo. It was just a large garden where, here and there, in the wilderness of an undergrowth, little pavilions were scattered. They were half in ruins, the discoloured walls were reflected in the stagnant waters of a lake. A hill rose in the centre; on the crest stood a round summer house and further on, a second wall disclosed another more intimate garden, in all probability in former times the residence of the proprietor.

It was decided to visit the grounds first, then to look at the pavilions. Tea in the summer house on the hill and afterwards a rest on the grass at the water's edge would pass the time until the dinner hour.

Chatours, who had already often visited the Wan Hei Lo offered himself as a guide. Every one followed him. Maugrais walked beside Miss de Frissonges. For a long time neither spoke. Then he murmured, "Look at this old corner of the East, it is like a faithful image of China in the past, the China that is disappearing."

She raised her pretty fair head, looked about her at the pavilions which seemed to tremble as if shaken by some strong scent escaping from the flowers hidden in the undergrowth, and said gaily, "Well, I am quite confident."

Maugrais seemed to understand the sense of her words, for he replied at once: "With you I am quite confident too."

They turned down a path and disappeared among the vegetation, keeping close to each other, like brother and sister strolling in their father's garden.

Old de Wolf, robust for his sixty years, followed them walking a little stiffly. He was proposing a plan for converting the Wan Hei Lo into a hotel for tourists. De Frissonges listened to him; precise and melancholy, he seemed to have left his youth behind him and forgotten the pleasures of the world in the Korean mines; only from force of habit was he continuing to lead the normal life of an engineer and a man of the world. M. de Beaurelois searched the undergrowth with his honest eyes and declared swarms of mosquitoes would descend on them at night-fall; Brixton, smoking a large cigar, stayed behind, tired of this garden which bored him, and concentrating all his ideas on some selfish and absorbing project, which the whole wide world was fated always to ignore. Mrs. Brixton approached the Baroness and took her gently by the arm. Blanche's elegant costume catching on every briar, was not at all suited to the age and decay around her. She had just sent Vladowsky from her; he had evidently paid her rather too crude a compliment, for her face was suffused with red and the indignation in her voice sounded almost sincere. He took to flight like a school boy in disgrace.

"I wish I could still blush like you, it is so becoming," said the American.

Her voice seemed melancholy; the Baroness noticed she looked absent and her eyes were dim.

"Let us go in here," she said, "and sit down for a bit."

They entered a small square courtyard, surrounded on three sides by narrow galleries, shaded by great trees whose trunks were covered with creepers.

"Do let's stay here, I am so tired."

They seated themselves on a heap of stones picturesquely arranged, forming grottos and recesses, Chinese fashion. Neither woman spoke. From a distance, the voices of the joyous band exploring the grounds reached them. The sun was sinking rapidly now, and a great calm, forerunner of twilight, spread over the earth. The Baroness had a vague impression that the American wanted to tell her something, but did not know how to begin. Scenting a confidence, she tried to encourage her.

"You seem preoccupied, even sad, tell me what is the matter?"

Mrs. Brixton looked at her for a minute, a melancholy expression in her eyes.

"Due allowances made, I feel, at the bottom of my heart, the same sadness that Christ must have experienced before deciding to mount Calvary or that Satan certainly must have felt before denying God."

She bowed her head and continued as if to herself: "The despairing courage of timid people has often been remarked upon; it is decidedly true. But on the other hand, the boundless fears and the disturbing weakness which so often paralyse the boldest, should also attract attention."

She was silent for a while, then she went on:

"As a tiny child, on Christmas Eve, when the doors, into the room where the tree was illuminated, were thrown open, I always wanted to burst into tears. And in after years, the day that the man I loved came to speak to my parents, I understood for the first time that death could be sweet."

Not knowing how to reply, Mme. de Beaurelois took her hand and kept it in her own. Mrs. Brixton raised her eyes, in them burnt a dull flame like a light at the bottom of a well.

"I swear if you took my arm this minute and led me wherever you wished, even the uttermost ends of the world, I would follow you without turning my head and I would spend the rest of my life trying to satisfy your slightest desire."

In the depths of her eyes the dull light flickered and died.

The Baroness said nothing. She did not quite understand what the American meant but felt instinctively she was passing through a painful crisis. Blanche contented herself with stroking the small nervous hand she held in her lap. Suddenly, Mrs. Brixton rose and walked up and down in the small courtyard. Now and then some English words escaped her. As she approached the cloisters, she seemed to grow faint or else a pang of despair must have shot through her for she grasped one of the wooden columns and leant her forehead against it; then she straightened herself, broke a twig off a tree near her and swished it in the air like a whip.

"Come," she said, "let us join the others."

She brushed down her dress, hitting it sharply with her cane.

As they joined the group, every one was getting ready for tea in the summer house. The American's face showed no trace of her recent emotion. She asked for the necessary ingredients for making cocktails and mixed them with such art and skill that every one congratulated her.

SILHOUETTES OF PEKING

The conversation skipped from one subject to another; from Yuan Shi Kai and his policy to a discussion on the outrageousness of the latest dress worn by Mrs. Ettinguer, the banker's wife; from the success young Porter of the Salt Administration had in the gymkhana to the scandal caused by the Brazilian Santafé being blackballed for the Peking Club.

"Yuan Shi Kai's strength lies in his being not only complete master in the North but also in the strong support he can command in Canton," said Brixton.

"Ettinguer is a Frankfort Jew and his wife is of the same race; that is the reason for their snobbishness," said Mme.

de Wolf. Being vaguely of Jewish extraction herself, she was inexorable on that subject.

"Porter wins all the steeplechases because he does not know how to ride," said Graziolli. "Obviously," he explained, "he does not realize the danger so he takes any sort of obstacles."

"The Brazilian Santafé was blackballed and rightly too," said Maxwell raising his voice, "it is time the air of the Peking Club was purified."

Count de Cordobas listened with an indulgent paternal smile. Never having experienced the joys of paternity, he was apt to treat them all as his dear prodigal children.

"Well, Mr. Chatours, what is your opinion on this question," asked Mme. Immersteht in the tone of a school master questioning a recalcitrant schoolboy.

Chatours, busy looking at Mme. de Beaurelois' plump white arms, turned to her. "Which question? I have heard three or four being discussed at once. If it is about Yuan Shi Kai and China's future, I don't mind confessing I am absolutely indifferent because I can see that China is irretrievably condemned to the noble fate of all old countries, decline and oblivion. It is as logical and as unavoidable as the death of an aged person. If you are discussing Mme. Ettinguer's dress I will tell you I do not blame her for her immodesty but for her ugliness. In the most ancient times of the sixth Egyptian dynasty under King Pepia I, the women covered their right breast with their tunics, leaving the left one bare. The young women exposed firm round breasts, the old ones, wrinkled and flabby: this excellent fashion certainly lasted longer than will the feeble creations and stupid conventions of our modern dressmakers. In olden days the beauty or ugliness of a dress was judged according to the shape and freshness of the exposed part. As for Porter and his laurels I will permit myself to guess that he wins races because his ponies are quicker than other people's. Finally we come to the regrettable case of the blackballed Brazilian; I am extremely sorry about it, because I have heard that Santafé is a great scoundrel. I have always had a

weakness for scoundrels and it would certainly have amused me more to see him about the Club than to meet at the bar the faces of the Anglo-Saxons which are always steeped in morality and branded with common sense."

This little speech aroused general indignation rather flattering to the orator. Only Mrs. Immersteht was annoyed and turned away looking for another victim.

The conversation followed the same channel for some time and no one noticed that night had fallen suddenly, as it always does in this country. In a small pavilion to one side, the boys, waking from their nap, could be heard hammering at cases and getting the crockery unpacked. The rattle of dishes, the tinkling of glasses and the popping of corks made an extremely Chinese noise. However, soon the voice of the cook could be distinctly heard above it; his sleeves rolled up, his apron on, he took command as a masterhand conscious of his importance. Fifteen minutes later, at the stone table made longer by the addition of a few stools, the places were laid. Chinese lanterns, hanging from the summer house beams, shed their light on a cloth covered with flowers, glass and silver. It all looked very inviting to the hungry company who sat down and began on the hors d'oeuvres.

The dinner was gay. Chatours, as usual, talked a lot; he was very animated. Beaurelois joked pleasantly with the ladies; Wolf, in a cheery mood, gave full rein to the robust enthusiasm of his sixty years, while Immersteht drowned the general chatter with his hearty laugh, which fell like a blow on the voices of the speakers. Maugrais sat between Mme. de Beaurelois and Melle de Frissonges, the former having Chatours on her right and the latter

Brixton on her left. Mme. Immersteht presided over the table from one end between de Frissonges and Wolf; at the other end Mme. de Wolf sat enthroned between Immersteht and Vladowsky. Beaurelois and Borioni occupied the remaining seats and Graziolli, sitting astride the bannisters, put his plate on the rail.

"You have been sent to the small table because you behaved so badly before dinner," said Mme. de Beaurelois.

All the smart set of Peking was assembled round the table. Only the de Maricourts were missing. They had left for the Shansi the day before. They had gone to look for a Han bronze they had been told about. It was supposed to be in the hands of a dealer in Taiyuanfu.

While both ends of the table were very gay and shouts of laughter rang through the air, falling in a torrent of gaiety, the centre remained calm and aloof.

Between Maugrais and Melle de Frissonges reigned one of those sweet eloquent silences known to lovers in the first moments of their happiness, when each look, each gesture and even each heart-beat are in tune. The girl bent over her plate seemingly entirely absorbed by its contents. She only turned her head to Maugrais to answer quietly some insignificant questions that were yet so full of meaning. Maugrais, observing her attentively, admired from an artist's point of view her delicate profile of ivory and mother of pearl. He took a psychological interest in discovering in her the timid confidence of the maiden who is giving herself and the generous conscious strength of a woman who is sacrificing herself. He admired the great heart hidden in this fragile little body. At the same time an immense tenderness crept over his whole being, an almost irrepressible desire to place his head, so heavy with dreams, in her lap. He wanted to seek shelter in her virgin yet maternal bosom. At this moment she raised her eyes. As if expressing aloud some idea that had come to them both she said with a shy, gentle glance at him:

"Yes, and those moments are never forgotten."

"Never," he echoed. Then he raised his eyes and saw Mrs. Brixton who was facing him. She was neither eating nor talking. She gazed at him fixedly, both her elbows on the table. It was not a brutal stab from a dagger that he received, but he felt a long sharp blade sinking stealthily into his heart. It reminded him of the twisted steel of the Malay knife which, with its poisoned tip and its bloodstained blade, slips into the victim's breast, spreading fire and death. He shuddered but could not take his eyes from hers. Many incoherent visions passed before his mental vision. At first he thought he was in a narrow cage descending rapidly a deep well, where twinkling lamps threw red shadows as of blood on coal-blackened walls. At the end of a long corridor the wild song of the Carmagnole mingled with the noise of picks and shovels.

This vision disappeared suddenly, like a mine plunged into darkness by the explosion of fire damp. Then under a burning noon-day sun, he saw the brilliant colours of a cuadrilla, heard the noisy ovations of a delirious mob, followed by the profound silence, impelled by the sight of blood soaking up the thirsty sand in an arena. An espada's beautiful and still youthful body was being carried away, the wide-opened astonished eyes seeming to fix themselves despairingly on an amphitheatre overflowing with people in holiday attire, and looking up at the immense deep blue sky.

Then a low bare roof, a strange tabernacle, dark clothes and hidden faces, long slender candles, throwing out a yellow light and a harsh guttural, imperative voice calling to the Prince of Darkness. Finally a horrible den, its light dimmed by opium fumes, a scent of bad wine spilt, where among drunken sailors, workmen in filthy blouses, and sickening prostitutes, a malevolent phantom of murder and lust seems to flit. Maugrais saw all this; he closed his eyes to keep the impression of these horrid visions under his lids. When a little later, he opened them, Mrs. Brixton had turned and seemed to be listening attentively to her neighbour's conversation. An indefinite period passed; Maugrais had a feeling that he was no longer at the Wan Hei Lo among this joyous company. He thought he had suddenly been carried away to some vague spot, so remote from this earth, that even the voice of hopes that kindled and sounds of suffering experienced here, came to him only as a distant echo or as a wave rising from the immense ocean to dissolve into creamy foam on the welcoming shore. Then he heard through the mist of his dream which was gradually fading away, the plaintive voice of the Baroness complaining softly to Chatours: "Dear friend, I feel you are no longer the same, you love another. I know that look of abstraction in the eyes of the man who is betraying me in his heart, those polite attentions of the lover who is thinking of abandoning me. Have the courage to break with me loyally; be frank and confess and although I may suffer a great deal, I think I shall find enough love in my heart to forgive."

SILHOUETTES OF PEKING

Maugrais did not catch the answer, but it must have been politely evasive for the Baroness gave a deep sigh and glanced wearily round the table. He followed that glance and examined the guests one by one as some one just arrived from a distant place and who wants to get once more into touch with his surroundings of the present moment. He saw de Wolf, very gay, passing his wrinkled hand through his abundant white locks, speechifying, plotting some new business, founding societies, breaking up Consortiums, joining by means of an electric railway the Bay of Biscay to the China Sea. He saw the wan, resigned smile on de Frissonges' face, who had some time ago buried his illusions in the goldfields of Northern Korea; he saw Mme. de Wolf, icy and stately, peeling a pear and offering a quarter to Vladowsky. The latter betrayed clearly by the way he was bending over the table that his hand had strayed far under the white skirts of his neighbour. By the fixed stare on Brixton's face, Jean knew that Vladowsky's manoeuvres had not escaped him, for he was watching, with the eye of an amateur, the effect of them on the always impassive and solemn countenance of Mme. de Wolf. He saw the paternal look of Cordobas, trying to forgive Mme. Immersteht her empty chatter as one forgives a baby for crying in church. He saw Beaurelois' honest eyes fixed on an annoying insect that he was trying to drive away without hurting. He saw old Borioni drowsing in his chair under the burden of his knowledge of Chinese and with closed eyes discovering that the 80,000 Chinese hieroglyphics he knew, had already been used for 3,000 years to express all the human passions experienced by this brilliant company.

Suddenly they all rose from the table, talking and laughing. Chatours proposed they should sit on the grass at the water's edge and tell stories. The boys could bring whiskey and soda. This idea pleased them all and they raced gaily down to the pool sleeping quietly at the foot of the hill. As soon as they were all settled, Mme. de Beaurelois, addressing herself to Borioni, asked him to tell them the history of Wan Hei Lo. Rumour said it was a romantic legend dating from Emperor Chien Lung's reign, but no one knew the details. The old Doctor tried to be let off at first, saying he had forgotten it, that he was tired. But they all insisted so he finally consented. There was a long silence. Then his pipe lit, his eyes staring into the undergrowth, he began:

"During his first campaign in Sungaria, the Emperor Chien Lung learnt the most dangerous and most unconquerable enemy of the Son of Heaven was the Chief of a powerful Mahometan tribe, Ali Arslan. His wife was supposed to be the most beautiful woman in Turkestan; all over the Central Tableland and even to the borders of Kukunor and Kansu she was known by the flattering appellation of 'Model of Beauty'. Chien Lung, who loved and appreciated the fair sex, sent word to his Chief of Staff Tchao Hui, that he would bestow special honours on him if the woman was brought captive to Peking. After a bloody struggle, Tchao Hui conquered the heroic tribe; Arslan was hanged on a gibbet erected before his deserted and looted camp; his family was put to death and his wife captured. Heralds proclaiming the great news were sent to the Emperor. Upon hearing it, he caused grand preparations to be made. A magnificent pavilion in the

Western Palace on the borders of Lake Nan Hai was put in order to receive the beautiful captive. It was arranged with all the splendour and luxury of an Eastern harem. The prisoner was renamed *Hsiang Fee*, signifying Sweet

Perfume, and afterwards she was always known as the Concubine of Sweet Fragrance. Scarcely had Tchao Hui reached Peking than he sought out his master to warn him of the great difficulty he had experienced in preventing

her from putting an end to her life. He had been obliged to watch her constantly. So Chien Lung went to visit his new Concubine in the Western Palace himself, accompanied by a numerous suite of women and eunuchs. Her great

beauty struck him immediately. Slender and fragile as a young palm tree she looked like a little girl. Her skin was extremely transparent and delicate, two serpents' eyes burnt in her restless nomad's head."

"When the Emperor drew near to kiss her, she sprang to her feet and drawing a short dagger, cried, 'Satan, do not dare to soil me by your touch'."

"From that day the Emperor, entirely conquered by his concubine's beauty, tried to tame her by every means in his power. The science of his advisers, the experience of his women were brought into consultation to win her heart. Hsiang Fee remained silent and unmoved. She only answered his too earnest entreaties by a look more icy and more cutting than the blade of her short dagger."

"Thus a year passed."

"One night some eunuchs came to tell the Emperor that the Concubine of Sweet Fragrance had lain on her couch all day with her head turned to the West crying bitterly. It was the Mahometan New Year. Chien Lung then understood the sickness of her Islam soul! He generously caused a mosque to be built exactly opposite the western Pavilion. Less than six months later, a beautiful white minaret faced the Pearl Moon Tower where Hsiang Fee loved to dream long hours away, her eyes towards the Kebla. Small white flat roofed houses, strange shops and bazaars grew up around the mosque. Soon an Eastern crowd appeared; none could tell from whence it came. An entirely Mahometan little town sprang up within a few feet of the Imperial Palace. Day and night the sad melodious voice of an old Mahometan priest called the faithful to prayer from his minaret. Under the burning Southern sun, women, their faces hidden, came from the houses of the shuttered windows and went down the narrow passages that were covered with matting and where turbaned merchants sold carpets, perfume, precious stones, weapons and sweetmeats."

"The Emperor had hoped this vision of a corner of her home land would make Hsiang Fee happier. The Concubine did indeed seem gentler and more resigned. But if her anger had abated, her sadness increased. The Emperor loved to pass long hours with her; he looked at her in silence. She lay on a Bokhara rug spread over a divan."

"Among the many cushions, she seemed overwhelmed with despair."

" 'Hsiang Fee', he would say sometimes, 'Tell me why you are so cruel. Don't you see I have entire kingdoms at my feet. Say the word and I will change the face of the earth'."

"She replied with scorn, 'It is written in the Eternal Book, God alone created the world, heaven and earth, He alone can change its face. There is but one God and Mahomet is His Prophet'."

" 'Hsiang Fee' he said, 'be kind and good to me. If I have caused your husband and family to be put to death it is because they were enemies of the State. And Confucius has said, 'destroy the enemy of social order'."

" 'Ignorant being,' answered Hsiang Fee, 'Do you not know there is no other reign but the Eternal's, the Greatest, the only One. As for your infidel States, they will be delivered into the fire and the Angel of Death will fly over your perishable cities'."

" 'Hsiang Fee, remember the words of the wisest of Men. Be patient and indulgent, do not render evil for evil'."

" 'The Prophet has said, the law of retaliation is commanded for murder; a free man for a free man, a woman for a woman. You killed my husband, you will perish by the sword'."

"A great uneasiness reigned over the Emperor's Court. He no longer busied himself with State affairs; even when seated on his throne he seemed lost in thought; his gaze turned to the West. His mother, the old Empress Niuhulu, who was more than 80 years of age and famed for her virtues, went to him one day and commanded him to send away the Concubine, Hsiang Fee. Chien Lung answered: 'I prefer death to separation from her.' And he seemed at that time to be seeking death."

"Talking one day to Hsiang Fee, he drew near the divan on which she rested. 'The Emperor Shun', he said, 'may certainly be considered the most virtuous and wisest man in history. He loved good but did not ignore evil. Between good and evil, he used to say, let us choose the golden mean and apply it to all we do. These are truly the words of a great sage.' "

" 'The words of a fool,' answered Hsiang Fee 'for the Prophet has said, despise the luke warm and the weak; desire only the unattainable, believe only in the impossible and yearn only for the infinite.' "

" 'Desire the unattainable, yearn for the infinite,' repeated Chien Lung slowly. Gently he slipped down on to the rug; burying his head in the cushions, he offered his back to the vengeance of her whom he had offended. A long silence followed. Then Chien Lung raised his head. Hsiang Fee was lending over him, her dagger motionless in the air. She looked like a snake poised ready to strike."

"Her whole being quivered like a young palm tree shaken by the warm breath of the desert."

" 'Well, strike,' said Chien Lung gently as if imploring a favour."

"But Hsiang Fee's arm fell heavily to her side and she said: `No, for your hour has not yet come'."

"For a few days the Emperor wandered like a madman in the immense grounds of the Forbidden City on the borders of the Three Lakes."

"A week later, the day of great sacrifice, Chien Lung went to the Temple of Heaven. After having presented his offerings, he was obliged, according to the ritual, to spend the night in the Long Fasting Hall. The old Empress sent her favourite eunuch to fetch the Concubine, Hsiang Fee. When she appeared she talked lengthily of her adored son, of the badly governed state, of the people who were dissatisfied and uneasy, of the war broken out in the South. She implored the young concubine to torture the Emperor no longer. It is even said that the haughty Niuhulu went so far as to throw herself at the feet of the Concubine. But Hsiang Fee raised her, and looking straight into the old woman's eyes, she bent her head and whispered something in her ear. The Empress gave a cry of great joy mingled with astonishment. But Hsiang Fee continued immediately. 'That is the reason why I would beg a last favour of your Majesty. I would die as died my husband and lord, hanging from a gibbet. The old Empress remained silent for a time as if searching in her heart the key to some riddle. Then this venerable lady whose name was composed of 18 characters praising her virtues, placed without a word a kiss of admiration on the Concubine's brow. Opening a door leading to the inner apartments, she bade her enter."

"The next morning, when Chien Lung returned to his Palace, his aged mother came to meet him. At once he understood the Irreparable had been accomplished."

"A gilt lacquered wood gibbet had been erected in the room next to the Empress; his beloved's fragile body was swinging from it. In her last sleep her small childish face had regained the calm and peace of the desert night. On her dainty lips forever closed a smile hovered, such as wear the angels guarding the gates of Paradise. Without a tear, Chien Lung knelt before her in dumb adoration; then rising, he laid on her pure cold lips his first kiss, the kiss of a brother and a lover."

"The funeral rites were as beautiful as those of a Princess of the Blood. The body of the Concubine of Sweet Fragrance was to be laid in a vault in the Hsi Ling Tombs."

"The procession set out towards evening, leaving the Imperial City by the Hsi Hua Men and going towards Pa Li Chuang and the western Hills. In spite of the custom of the country, the Emperor refused to use his chair, but dragging his splendid Imperial robes in the dust of the roads, followed on foot the coffin borne by 72 serving men. Dead tired and worn out by grief, he stopped the procession some way from the city walls and ordered a night's rest in the Wan Hei Lo Palace. It was here, in these grounds, amid this wild vegetation and these tumbling pavilions that the Imperial procession passed the first night on its way to the Hsi Tombs."

"The coffin was placed in a small isolated pavilion on the other side of the lake. The Princes, wives and concubines passed the night in the second enclosure; the ministers and generals were in the pavilion near the entrance tower. The reminder of the people went to the neighbouring village. The Emperor refused to rest but insisted on spending the night by the coffin of his beloved."

Dr. Borioni rose and with his unlighted pipe he pointed out the dilapidated pavilion drooping over the dark water.

"Alone that night by the bedside of his adored one, his head, heavy with the destiny of a whole country, rested on the coffin. Was he speaking softly to her of his love, great as the world, strong as death? Or was he imploring her as he watered with his scalding tears the cedar wood and the rich brocades, to forgive him now death had robbed him of her beautiful body, and not to pursue her vengeance after death? In the silence of the night did he pronounce words that were wild and great, tragic and sacrilegious, or did he perhaps commit deeds that the blind and stupid world would condemn? No one will ever know. But when at early dawn, the procession started, crossing the old stone bridge over the canal, the Emperor had become white as snow and his gaze, formerly so proud and domineering, contained sharp flames and the blue lights of a visionary."

Dr. Borioni said no more, and his thin outstretched arm pointed in the direction where 150 years ago, the Imperial funeral had passed on its way to the Western Tombs.

Every one remained silent and it seemed as if the very soul of Wan Hei Lo had suddenly revealed itself to these people so greedy of impressions and pleasures.

"Wan Hei-Lo, Wan Hei Lo!" repeated Chatours as if he wished to inhale the drugged and morbid scent of this Eastern name.

But suddenly a figure loomed out of the night. It was Mrs. Brixton. She had risen and was standing up motionless. Slender and fragile she looked like a young girl and, in the eyes of her friends still under the influence of the story of the heroic concubine, she seemed the incarnation of the dead woman. Without a word, slowly and stiffly she walked automatically towards the pavilion where Hsiang Fee's coffin had lain. She looked like a somnambulist walking alone in the night.

Silent and resigned, Maugrais rose and followed her. They crossed the little bridge over the water and found themselves opposite the old pavilion. Half in ruins, the door open into the darkness, it was infested with bats. An odour of death, of putrefaction came from these abandoned walls, a whiff of the irrevocable past floated in the air. It was like the entrance to a tomb. On the threshold Mrs. Brixton paused. Maugrais drew nearer, he saw she shivered as if with fever and again the vision of a slender palm tree shaken by the warm breath of the desert flitted before his eyes. He seized her in his arms, she turned to him all at once, supple and soft like a snake ready to strike.

"Lucy," he breathed passionately.

"Yes," she answered putting her arms around him, "Yes, your hour has come."

A deadly silence fell on Wan Hei Lo. Only the shrill cry of a toad from the water gave a tragic note to the night. A strong scent of marshy reeds and poisonous weeds filled the air; from the stagnant water rose an unhealthy mist which, floating hither and thither, formed strange human shapes as if the phantom of the concubine, Hsiang Fee, followed by a ghostly retinue, was visiting once more this park of love and death.

Gradually the crowd broke up into groups or tête-à-tête, in the summer house, at the water's edge, on the ruined steps of the small pavilions. The night was so beautiful that no one thought of sleeping. Here and there through the holes in the walls the shadows of the "boys," settling the camp beds could be seen. Lights flickered and from afar came the mournful cries of the night watchman protecting the orchards from beggars and thieves.

Mme. de Beaurelois had long been attempting to get Chatours away alone with her; but he had displayed as much astuteness in avoiding this tête-à-tête as she had in seeking it. He had finally attached himself to Mr.

de Frissonges and was questioning him about Korea before the Japanese occupation. The old engineer at first answered in monosyllables, but he soon warmed to the subject as it called up memories of the country where he had spent his youth.

"Ancient Seoul," said he, "sleeping at night in its valley between the hills like a child in its cradle! The air is so soft that the breeze blowing about you, covers you with scented caresses, like a bunch of flowers thrown by a woman as she passes. And those white shapes of the Koreans as they flit by! They seem to come from a fairy tale in which ghosts walk smiling among men. Poor dear Korea, Kingdom of the Calm Morning, country of indolence and lust, of dreams and gloom, where art thou, sad white vision of the East?"

The Baroness, taking shelter by the Count's side, had seized his beringed hand and was talking to him of death. "I would like three words engraved on my tomb. Thou hast loved. What would you like on yours?"

"I don't know," replied Cordobas. "Perhaps, Thou hast lived."

A long silence ensued; then all at once he began to talk, his head thrown back, his gaze fixed on the far off stars. He spoke as if in a dream. "After my death I do not wish my body washed with water, nor embalmed with precious ointments, but I ask that it should be cleansed with fine old Burgundy . . . And that is my first wish. I want no candles nor incense placed before my bier but I ask that opium may be burnt so that blue smoke-spirals of the soothing drug may float over my body and that is my second wish. At my funeral, let a choir of boys sing the *De Profundis*, so that the warm alto of the breaking voice may mingle with the clear treble of the child. Let an introit of sheer purity ring out before the Lord for me . . . and that is my last wish."

It was past midnight. Lucy and Maugrais were still sitting on the threshold of Hsiang Fee's pavilion. The American's face bore not the slightest trace of triumph nor of satisfied desire. She was gentle and grave as if an unavoidable event had come to pass in which she had only taken part because impelled by fate's irresistible force. Maugrais talked warmly to her for a long time. Certain corners of his being, hidden from him so far, had been revealed tonight. He had found himself again in the unwholesome and burning passion that assailed him. Everything shapeless had materialized; even hazy dreams dating back to far distant childhood's years had simply and suddenly become clear. Doubt had left him. Scruples had vanished; the secret, most intimate recesses of his heart, which up to now he had not dared to probe, seemed all at once quite clear, as if a light had dropped to the bottom of a vault; all his life appeared as a venturesome race towards this final unfolding. His eyes haggard, his voice hoarse, he seemed delirious and torrents of words tumbled from his lips.

"Again and again and for ever I must say to you, I love you, love you, love you. I want to tell you that as a little child I already loved you. When in the sunlit fields I chased the dainty butterfly and when I played with my ball, tossing it into the air, towards the blue sky, I loved you. As a young boy, I already loved you; bending over my Greek lesson, translating Homer and the learned Xenophon, I loved you. As a young man, greedy for love and longing for what life would hold, I loved you. During my travels, in my dreams, gentle or wild, I loved you. As my youth leaves me, I love you still with the anguish of a heart growing old, of a heart that is dying yet burns with a crueller and more devastating flame than the hottest fire that ever kindled round me. Listen to me, I love you, love you, love you. Falling at your feet, I shed tears for my wasted life, my misspent life, my useless life; in its despair, my bleeding heart, all steeped in love, calls to you. My beloved, I know that centuries are passing over our heads like a flight of birds flying to happier climes, but I want to stay here, motionless, tied to your material being, nailed to your sinful soul, dragging through endless ages the weight of my crime and the folly of my love. I want every thing to perish, to die, to vanish. I thirst for the abyss of the dark night, to love you no longer with the love that is worse than death, for I love you, love you, love you, love you, and my love flames like Lucifer himself come straight from Hell."

Millions of stars twinkled in the dark and solemn sky, speaking to each other through the infinite space in a mute luminous language of flashes of light. They called up the memory of ages buried forever in the unfathomable mystery of the past and announced the coming of centuries of unrelenting time.

And all appeal from Here Below was unanswered. No sound reached the bottomless pit where for countless years human pain and misery had been swallowed up, where oceans of blood and floods of tears will be shed until the end of all time.

Lying on the grass his eyes fixed on the dark firmament, Maugrais was now quite still and the immensity of his love soared in communion with the infinite.

SILHOUETTES OF PEKING

After a sleepless night, Miss de Frissonges rose; her face was pale and her features looked drawn. Her neighbour, Mme. de Wolf still slept on her camp bed; the sun had hardly crossed the horizon above the yet sleeping city of Peking.

She sat for a while on the stretched cloth of her narrow bed, her hands folded on her lap, her eyes fixed on the paper that replaced the panes on the windows of her room. A large black spider hung down from the roof by a thread so fine that it appeared to be hanging from the air and she said softly: "Spider in the morning, great sorrow." Then rising, she dressed with haste to precede the others. When she left the pavilion, all was still quiet and she could have fancied herself alone in the Wan Hei Lo. She went into the garden. Her first impression was one of surprise at finding nothing changed, at seeing the old fir trees still as dark and dignified round the small tumble-down pavilions, and at feeling a great calm that spread itself over the green covering of Nature. The summer house struck her especially, it was abandoned now, only an empty bottle lay forgotten on the stone table. Her eyes sought the water and the pavilion opposite, towards which Mrs. Brixton and Maugrais had gone, to appear no more last evening. There was something severe and simple in the unadorned walls of the pavilion, its roof with upturned angles, pointing to the sky. The building had its back to the lake and to the summer house, as if it wished to turn away, annoyed at being watched.

Miss de Frissonges felt plainly how simple are the important things in life and how very indifferent Nature is to the drama of humans. She went to the gate, sighing deeply. The country looked fresh and radiant stretching out gaily under the yet timid rays of the sun. There was such a contrast between the healthy strength of this life just awaking and the death that filled her heart. The birds were twittering overhead, the cry of the cicada rang out. Voices from a village across the marshes reached her; a pony grazing peacefully on a bank raised his head, snorted and resumed his absorbing occupation. The impression she had had of Nature's indifference to human suffering increased, a clear feeling of the complete isolation of human beings struck her forcibly. "We are born alone, we live alone and we die alone," she said to herself, "And everything else, nature, men and beasts, is only the accidental frame in which useless human life moves and struggles."

A violent desire to lie down on the still damp, dewy grass seized her; a desire to lay her head on the ungrateful earth, to vanish and to melt into oblivion. She was now walking across country towards the Mongol Tombs, dragging her riding skirt through the damp grass. The desire to sink into oblivion was so great that her heart throbbed painfully as if the hand of death had already touched her. She came up to a solitary hut, surrounded by a few trees and she suddenly saw near her, a shapeless black form wriggling in the grass. Mechanically she approached and saw it was a big black sow; it was lying full length there breathing heavily; its enormous belly rose and fell like the bellows of a forge and quite close to her, something small and indefined moved about like larvae attacking a large body.

The sow, overwhelmed by the happiness and the pain of her maternity, was farrowing before her sty. Her snout buried in the ground, she heeded naught around her, the supreme effort of her being was applied to bringing fresh life into the world. And before this picture of eternal fecundity, this clear sunshiny morning, the girl felt so violent a need of happiness, so sharp a desire to live spring up in her bruised heart, that, seized with giddiness her legs gave way beneath her and she sank to the ground, her whole body shaken by a storm of sobs which ended in a flood of tears. Quite close to her, the sow was still breathing heavily, indifferent, to everything but the one object of her dull life, now realized in the bosom of Mother Earth, while overhead the sun, now high in the Heavens, advanced triumphantly to the conquest of the day.

Half an hour later, Miss de Frissonges returned to Wan Hei Lo, had her pony saddled and rode slowly along the road to Peking. She was alone, her pale, thin face was lit up by a calm smile of resigned pain and over there near the Chinese hut the black sow was sleeping calmly, her snout buried in the ground and beside her played her little ones, pink and white like petals from a large flower sent by Nature as the supreme gift of maternity achieved.

Almost at the same hour, Maugrais left Wan Hei Lo and paused on the old stone bridge. Some naked urchins were playing in the yet cool water and their shrill cries rose above the noise of their splashing. Tanned and droll, they looked like large brown frogs.

Maugrais crossed the bridge and climbed the bank. The green plain of Peking lay before him, stretching out gaily to the Western Hills. However, he did not linger to contemplate this smiling landscape he loved so much. He walked on, his head bent, buried in thought.

His whole being was submerged in such intense and complicated feelings that he had an urgent need of solitude. A giddiness seized him each time he searched his heart, an instinctive fear possessed him before which, terrified, he retreated. All his life he had been seeking happiness, and at last he had found it, under the skies of a beautiful summer night. Did he then fear, at dawn, to have grasped but a shadow?

Was he not like a man who, tired of life, had thrown himself into the sea and diving into unfathomable depths, suddenly opens his eyes and sees rising from the bottom of the ocean, strange gigantic plants, silent fish with greedy eyes glide by him? He had only sought for oblivion and death and he had discovered an unknown underseas life!

"I love her, I am quite certain," he said aloud. "I have found untold treasure in my great love for her." Then without any apparent reason, a small picture of his past life came to his memory. It had happened in Burmah, he was only visiting the gardens of a Palace in Mandalay. A little girl was working among the fantastic and exotic flowers there. He stopped to watch her and perceived on her finger the most beautiful ruby he had ever seen. Even in this country of gems he was surprised to see such a costly and lovely stone on the finger of a peasant. He drew near to examine it closely. And then he discovered it was a great drop of blood.

"This naughty cactus pricked me," said the child raising her soft, exotic eyes. Her whole bronze face lit up with the calm smile of the East.

Maugrais was now walking quickly through the fields, crossing villages, passing by tombs, jumping ditches and sunken road; he was madly racing away from Peking in his haste to be alone in the brilliant sunlit country. Some peasants saw him pass through Yuan Tsai Tsung and continue towards Tsai Pu Chuang. He was seen going by the Guan Ding Hsi tombs; some small children cried, *Tah Laoie* after him as his mournful figure appeared behind the old neglected Pa Li Chuang Pagoda. He went on, his head held low, waving his whip as if pursued by the ghost of Peking and attracted by the joyous sight of the Hills looming large to the West and peopled with ruined temples. There was the energy of despair in his resolute air; he was making the last effort of an already broken spirit. This tragic figure in its rush to the West recalled the race of a great captain who, abandoned by his retreating army and seeing the battle decidedly lost, advances alone towards the frontier, brandishing his conquered sword in a supreme effort to grasp the victory eluding him.

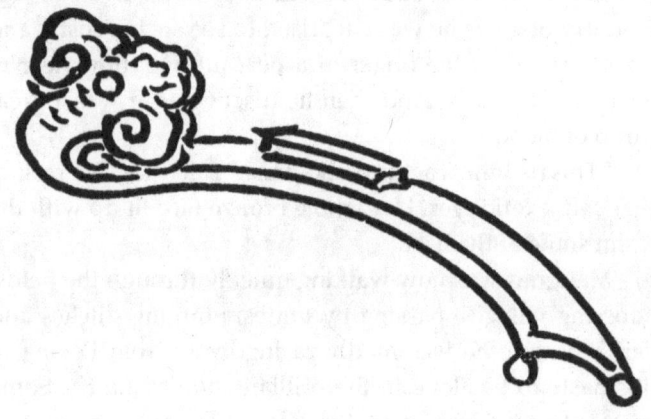

CHAPTER VIII

CHATOURS had now been Marchioness Ting's lover for about a month. She was a little Chinese lady, born in London where her father had been Ambassador. Having lived for a dozen years in the different European Capitals she had been an object of a curiosity forming the basis of her successes there.

Her husband had been sent by the Wai Chiao Pu on a mission to the United States to settle the emigration question. During his absence, he had left her in Peking. She consoled herself easily, and was always to be seen at the Hotel de Pekin Saturday dances, where the people usually found there had nicknamed her "the Merry Widow." She was said to be of easy virtue and to have had many adventures. Her origin was Manchu; her height was superior to that of most of her race and her slight figure made her appear even taller. Her eyes slanted but little and her skin was only moderately tinted; she spoke English and French with equal fluency having learnt them during her father's sojourn in Europe. She could even dance the tango and at first sight gave the impression of being a half caste from Macao.

One evening, Chatours was amusing himself watching her turn in the arms of a young secretary from the Foreign Office; recently returned from some Legation abroad, he was trying unsuccessfully to master the complicated steps of the Argentine dance. A friend, seeing he was interested, had introduced him. The Marchioness, flattered at having attracted the attention of this young man supposed to be rather unsociable, had made herself extremely amiable. Amused by her chatter, Chatours had accepted an invitation to tea. He had gone again several times, visiting her in her German-colonial Palace near the Bell Tower. One day, pursued by Mme. de Beaurelois's reproaches, he had succumbed to temptation and had justified his friend's jealousy.

He had led the attack boldly and his adversary had only defended herself for pure form's sake easily accepting her defeat.

Their first meeting had left him under the impression of being with a delicate, little, fragile person whose movements were insipid but whose figure was pleasing. An unsuspected passion had been an agreeable surprise to him and helped to make him forget Blanche with rapidity. For her well regulated and quiet intimacy began to seem very tasteless to a palate now accustomed to something spicier.

The first period passed, he still felt real pleasure in caressing that pretty body with its amber velvet skin which quivered under his touch. Her rather childish chatter still amused him; he liked to make her tell him impressions of Europe. On her side, she asked the pretty "foreign devil" as she called him, for details of the sentimental life of young men in Paris.

Up to now the Marchioness had always received Chatours in the large European house she occupied during her husband's absence. The furniture too loud and flashy, made the place look like one of those hastily built temporary palaces at an exhibition; there were too many electric lamps and mirrors. Chatours had told her so one day jokingly and had insisted he should be shown her father-in-law's house; he had heard Prince Luo owned some wonderful things.

She had always avoided consenting, saying a Chinese interior was not interesting, and that the Prince lived a very retired life. But tired of arguing and unable to resist any longer she had promised to tell him of Chatours' desire. Finally to-day he was going with her at five o'clock to call on the old man.

He had scarcely been more than a few minutes in the little boudoir, furnished like a hotel for tourists where he had been waiting, when she appeared.

Contrary to her usual custom, she had abandoned her tailor made suit and was wearing Chinese robes. A short dark silk skirt, disclosed her slender ankles, a kind of tunic buttoned at one side and made of light coloured material, outlined discreetly her bust and fell loosely a little below the waist. The collar, slightly starched and open in front, hid the nape of her neck; she wore a large pearl rosace at each side of her head like the ornaments seen on Assyrian statues. They made a white spot against her tightly drawn black hair. She wore no other jewels save round her right wrist, a circlet of jade, deep green like an emerald.

"You look delightful," said Chatours kissing her hand. "Why on earth do you usually wear European clothes? You see how wrong it is not to wear the national costume. I am so sorry I did not come to China in the time of the Empire. I should have loved to see you wearing your hair Manchu style with the multi coloured enamel bar raising it skillfully. Fancy you, draped in a ceremonial robe of gaily patterned *kosseu*! You would have appeared to me as a great Empress of whom I should have been the most faithful subject and slave."

"You are joking, my friend. You would have found me perfectly ridiculous. How can you compare your delightful Paris fashions to our horrible garments? But let us go or we shall be late."

The motor was at the door, they went swiftly to the North of the town in the direction of the Yellow Temple.

The Palace in which the old Prince resided had long been a family possession. Emperor Kang Hsi had bestowed it as a gift on an ancestor of the present owner in recognition of services rendered.

After having driven for a quarter of an hour down Hatamen the chauffeur turned to the left, then he stopped, they had reached their destination.

As is usually the case in the houses of princes, two imposing stone dragons guarded the entrance. The roof over the door was slightly curved; on the ends were earthenware animals of all sorts, like unicorns. Opposite the opening was a piece of wall built exactly in front of the door, thus respecting the letter if not the spirit of the Chinese etiquette which forbids the commoner to let his unworthy gaze rest on the door of a house sheltering the great of the world. On each side, in a sort of rack, red halberds with horse hair tails at the top also indicated the high rank of the old Prince.

The *kai men ti* hurriedly came to the door of the car. He took respectfully the card Chatours handed to him. Holding it to his head as a sign of respect he hastened to announce the visitors. The young man and his companion waited outside in the car. He soon returned however, making signs for them to follow him. Chatours and the Marchioness crossed a series of courtyards all decorated differently. Cleverly disposed pieces of rock making a landscape and miniature mountains ornamented the first, then the scene changed, green plants covered the ground, lace-like marble bridges joined the banks of a small canal, whose waters almost vanished under the large flat lotus leaves, their straight stems growing skywards, and holding out as offerings, the white or pink petals just showing the emerald green pistil in their centre. A last door passed, the couple found themselves in a carved wood gallery which led to the Reception Hall.

As the young man mentioned his surprise at the round about road they had been brought, his companion explained this winding way was necessary, according to

SILHOUETTES OF PEKING

a superstition the Chinese architects are obliged to take into account, for the house must be protected against evil spirits. These evil spirits always move in a straight line and would soon take away everything of value if the openings were facing one another all the way through; but the slightest bend is sufficient to debar them so it is simple to mislead them. What is lost in symmetry is gained in safety.

The *kai men ti* preceded them. He stopped and with one hand he raised the curtain before him. It was made of matting and decorated with gilt nails. The host, as a sign of respect came forward and made as if he too, would hold the light hanging.

He was a tall old man with fine features and a slender figure. A small white beard on his chin made his face look even thinner than it was. His eyelids were heavy, but a bright glance filtered through them, sufficing to animate his face. His complexion of a yellow hue gave one the impression of an old ivory statue. He bowed to Chatours, bidding him welcome; then still showing in the usual way the joy this visit caused him, he led him to the end of the room and made Chatours sit on the ceremonial *kang* in the place of honour on the left. Strictly observing the etiquette the young man resisted, insisting the old man should sit beside him.

Meanwhile the Marchioness seated herself on one of the Cantonese wood chairs which are always beside a *kang*. A large piece of marble is inlaid in the back of these chairs. As Chatours' Chinese was not fluent enough to keep the conversation going, she translated as he spoke.

The furniture of this room was fairly quiet. At the side

opposite the entrance, a large mirror of the Ch'ien Lung period reached to the ceiling. It was framed in ironwood and rested on a carved foot. In the centre, on a round table, the usual clock of European make had pointed doubtless to the same hour for many years. In a corner on a stand between two artificial plants with leaves and flowers of coloured stone, stood a horned shaped tinted glass vase. Its blue and gold design betrayed its foreign origin. Spittoons were symmetrically placed before the chairs, indiscreet signs of a praise-worthy attention to hygienics.

On the paper walls, where holes betrayed the curiosity of the servants, whose shadows moved about behind the thin screen, some paintings, appropriate to the season, were hanging. They represented landscapes and birds in beautiful Ming colours.

A silent-footed boy brought scented tea; the old man filled his guest's cup himself and waited for Chatours to drink first.

Chatours who knew the sacred rites of etiquette began by the customary compliments on the Prince's health.

"I am glad," he said, "to see you enjoy a robust old age. The years, while bringing you wisdom have not lessened your strength."

"Alas," said the old man, "I have spent 70 useless years."

"You slander yourself, your merit is great and every one is aware of the many qualities you have displayed in the interests of the State."

"Yes, eyes have been cast at my humble person, but I was not worthy of the notice. It was wrong to confide for so many years the position of Salt Administrator in the Northern Provinces to me. I know nothing and I still have everything to learn. I am ignorant of all foreign science whereas you, *Cha Ta Yen*, in spite of your youth, you have a great deal of experience and your knowledge is boundless."

While they were exchanging these compliments, the Prince played all the time with two ivory balls. He held them in his right hand and rolled them about to keep his tapering fingers supple.

Mechanically he stopped.

"I have read," he said, "in the Chinese papers that very learned Europeans have discovered the means of curing a great many ailments. Is it true that it is possible for an old man to regain the vigour of his youth or for a man exhausted by disease to obtain new rich blood?"

It took Chatours some seconds to grasp that his host was alluding to human grafting and to the transfusion of blood. He explained to the best of his ability that it was at last possible for great scientists to perform these wonderful things and that in many cases such operations had saved the patients' life, when even the most powerful remedies, such as powdered tigers' claws, so dear to the Chinese doctors, had failed.

While he was giving these explanations, the old man could not conceal his astonishment. He listened to Chatours attentively, his head turning first to the right then to the left as if he could thus follow the young man's words with more ease. Stroking his small white beard, the polite and amiable expression he had worn since the beginning of the conversation left his face and he remained lost in thought, for some time.

Then a boy brought him a water pipe with a long bent mouth piece; having filled the little bowl with his own hands, he took from the servant a lighted paper spill which at one end was burning slowly and holding it to the pipe, he drew a long breath making the flame leap up. Then he offered it to his guest with the usual compliments.

Just then the curtain against the door was raised and two young men entered. The old man introduced them to Chatours, they were his sons. They were clothed in European fashion and wore with ease their tussore silk suits made for them by the English tailor in Morrison street. Their soft collars, indispensable in the summer time, were fastened under their ties with a gold safety pin, giving them an Anglo-Saxon air. However, this was modified by their large gold rimmed spectacles, the only concession they made to ancient Chinese customs.

After the habitual polite phrases, the elder one said in French: "I was educated in France. As you know, during the last years of Kuang Hsü's reign, many of the young generation went abroad to study. Our father, yielding to our earnest wish, allowed my brother and myself to go also to learn something of modern civilization. For four years, I studied in Paris at the School of Political Science and at the Law College. My brother went to Japan for two years and studied railroad construction at the Osaka Engineering College. Afterwards he went to the United States to finish. We returned almost three years ago. My brother is in the ministry for Communications and I am secretary at the Foreign Office." Then he smiled and continued. "Look, you have a picture of the country before your eyes. My father is of the old School, the Mandarin of Li Hung Chang's time, we two represent 'Young China' as they say in the magazines."

"And I must confess we are not always of the same opinion on all questions. But is not that the case everywhere even in Europe, where the conservatives, horrified at anything new, struggle against the progressive party."

While the young man was speaking his brother was translating briefly to their father the sense of the conversation. Giving his pipe to the servant behind him, the old man spoke: "You see we only suspected the superiority of your knowledge when you came with your great men-of-war armed with long distance guns and settled among us. Even then it took us many years to realize we must adopt your ways and it was only when Japan, who had already modernized itself a little, took Korea after defeating our navy and our army, that we finally understood the necessity of assimilating ourselves. But by then I was already too old. I had to limit myself to sending my sons to steep themselves in those sciences which my mind could never grasp. When a building is finished, it is difficult, not to say impossible, to change the plans. But while the building is but little above the level of the ground, there is time to alter it. Their brain was still capable of adapting itself to the new ways, mine was already fully developed."

Chatours nodded approval.

"It was anyhow a wise thing to allow the future generation to participate in the benefits you have not been able to profit by yourself and I admire your wisdom."

"It is small credit to us," replied the Prince, "Many others have done the same thing. However all is not for the best. The young people are often very presumptuous, those who have lived abroad have forgotten there, I am afraid, the teachings of our old philosophers. The immortal Lao Tzu has said: 'Without leaving home it is possible to know the whole world, it is not necessary to look out of the window to see one's way to Heaven; the more one travels the less one can learn; without moving one can know; without looking one can see and it is unnecessary to work in order to obtain results'."

"The new generation sometimes seems to lose sight of this fundamental truth. Too often they despise the experience of old men who have studied the things of the past. And we cannot attempt to abolish all at once a civilization of thousands of years and put in its place, without any transition, new ideas brought without alteration from countries which have lived and progressed without coming into contact with us."

"China also has a glorious past; its Emperors of the powerful Tsing dynasty made Asia quake, and Ch'ien Lung, the last of its conquerors, made the name of the Chinese respected even to the far off borders of Turkestan. Our own history can therefore give us examples for the governing of our immense Empire which contains more than four hundred million souls."

The old man was getting animated; he no longer played with the two ivory balls so similar in colour to his slender parchment-looking hands. His eyes shone between his half closed lids and he continued as if to himself.

"Misfortune will fall on those who have too much confidence in themselves; they cannot escape the fate awaiting the presumptuous. As the old Master said: 'He who is satisfied with himself does not shine; he who boasts has no merit, he who sets himself up above the others will never rise. He is like the remains of a meal or like a tumour on a limb, an object of universal disgust, and those who know will turn aside from him'."

As if ashamed of having shown his feelings and betrayed some of his intimate thoughts, the Prince said no more, then his eyes wandered and having regained his impassiveness, he began to play once more with the little ivory balls which rattled between his gnarled fingers.

Silent up to now, the younger son began to speak. "Obviously," he said, "our ideas shocked the people accustomed to the old regime; of course we younger ones should consider the existing state of affairs and therefore we can only slowly and cautiously introduce foreign civilization into China. Our father is right to put the younger generation on its guard against too great ambition. Nevertheless we must not be intimidated by the obstacles, put in our path through ignorance and custom; we must make the best of things and even if we should upset centuries-old prejudices, our ideas will finally triumph. Yes, we shall end by giving China a modern administration which will permit it to realize all its riches and to develop its resources. Besides the situation in which we find ourselves is not new. Does not England, for example, like other European countries, hover between two parties one attempting to arrest all progress the other struggling to precipitate things. Our father represents the former my brother and myself the latter. As for the old national philosopher, he certainly left us immortal principles, drawn from the wisest sources, but he should not be our only guide, for certain of his sayings are the absolute reverse to progress as for instance, those founded on the theory of inaction: 'Practise inactivity, be content to do nothing'."

The conversation dragged a few minutes more. Chatours understood it was now time to go. He rose. The Prince, smiling and polite, accompanied him to the door; according to Chinese etiquette, he made as though to go as far as the second courtyard. But the young man, following the customary protocol, refused this honour and some minutes passed in the exchange of protestations. Finally giving in as if with regret, the old man allowed himself to be persuaded; he bowed for the last time to his visitor. His two sons, less stiff, shook hands heartily with him.

As his motor went rapidly through the streets, Chatours thought of the scene in which he had just taken a part. The amiable old man personified ancient China; he was the great Empress, Tse Hsi's attendant. Then he had a vision of the mandarins, their magnificent robes iridescent under the sun's kisses and their ceremonial hats adorned with peacock's feathers, begging an audience of the Son of Heaven.

Those days had past. No more flowered robes embroidered with dragons, no more carrying chairs, the commonplace morning coat and the scanty evening clothes had driven away the old ceremonial garments. But could these young men almost at their ease in their European clothes really change the state of affairs and restore the Golden Age as did their predecessors in the Land of the Rising Sun?

His thoughts had wandered thus far, when the Marchioness, annoyed by his long silence, began to talk, "Little Foreign Devil, do you remember Mr. Li, one of my admirers of whom you were rather jealous? Well, you can now be reassured, he has returned to the Honan, his native province."

"Indeed, why is he in disgrace?"

"Oh, nothing very important. As secretary at the Presidency he 'squeezed' too much and they were obliged to remove him, but he will certainly be in favour again within a few months."

Chatours smiled and seeking no longer to arrange China's future, he chattered to the dear little doll seated beside him.

SILHOUETTES OF PEKING

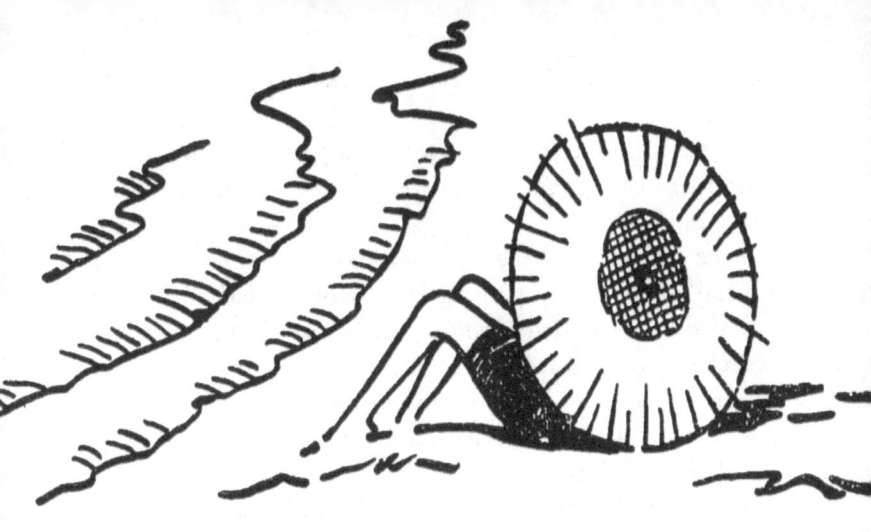

CHAPTER IX

THE intense heat had already driven to the sea side those people who were not obliged to stay in Peking. Mme. de Beaurelois, declaring she needed rest and quiet, had deserted Pei Ta Ho for Shan Hai Kwan this year. The latter place was an unpretentious family resort and seemed better suited to the state of mind into which her latest sentimental adventure had plunged her. However, not wishing to find herself quite isolated, she had sung the praises of the place to her set, and nearly every one followed her there.

On the fine sands washed by the waves of a sea, almost always calm, the merry company, as it had been nicknamed, met morning and evening. Blanche, in love with the picturesque, had refused to live in one of the villas on the coast. With the buildings belonging to the English, French and Italian guards, they formed the entire European village. She settled herself in a large temple some way from the sea, but overlooking the river; it had a broad terrace shaded by a few trees where she could pass the evenings.

The temple had been abandoned some years ago by the priests. Only painted idols with grimacing faces recalled the primitive purpose of the place. Some Chinese merchants bought it to let to bathers during the summer months. One part of the building, roughly repaired, the rooms whitewashed afresh each season, was large enough to shelter the easily satisfied tenants, amused by the prospect of a lengthy camping out holiday. Of course camp beds were indispensable and the furniture comprised only the absolutely necessary.

Mme. de Beaurelois had taken the whole temple with the Immerstehts. It could hold about fifteen people. The meals were in common, but except at lunch and dinner where every one met, they all amused themselves quite independently.

This week Blanche had as her guests the de Wolfs, Graziolli and Miss de Frissonges whose father, recalled to Peking on business, had left her there. The Immerstehts' guests were Dr. Borioni and a young Dutchman, Van Axel, just come from the South, where, as Councillor for irrigation affairs, he had been to survey some hydraulic works for the Chinese Government.

After dinner every one assembled on the terrace. A single lamp placed on the stone table gave out a dim light and in the semi darkness the men's cigars glowed red on the faces in the shadows.

No one spoke, they were all very pensive; comfortably lazy after their meal and ashamed to disturb the silence of the night. The only sounds were the far off murmur of the waves as the tide rose on the near-by beach and the noise of the stream at the foot of the temple as it rustled through the reeds on the banks. A low-flying sea gull went through the air uttering plaintive cries. That was sufficient to break the charm. The powerful Immersteht who never wasted much time on thought, even when digesting his meals, rose suddenly, fearful of growing fat, from the wicker chair where he had been smoking quietly.

"You know, my dear," he said to Mme. de Beaurelois, "you were wrong not to accompany us on our excursion to-day. The heat was not excessive and we reached the Hunchback Temple without tiring ourselves. We had a wonderful view from above. I left Miss de Frissonges and the men to go on horseback and I went on foot taking the short cuts."

"But you must be dead tired," said Mme. de Wolf, "how can you still move about?"

"Good Heavens," answered the Collossus, "I can't take any credit for that, it is just a question of training."

And going up to Graziolli he started a long argument with him on the merits of Swedish exercises for keeping the body supple and the muscles in good condition.

Van Axel took the empty glass Miss de Frissonges was holding in her hand and put it on the table. For a few moments he looked at her; he had quite recently come to Peking; up to now he had lived in Shanghai and Canton; he had arrived here at the beginning of the summer just before every one scattered.

Mme. de Beaurelois took him at once under her wing. This shy young man with kind blue eyes, frank face and fair hair won all hearts from the start. Blanche made him promise to spend his week ends with her and nearly every week saw him at Shan Hai Kwan. During the excursion to the Hunchback Temple he rode beside Miss de Frissonges talking to her when the pace slackened. Graziolli and the other men annoyed her with their chatter, but he did not bore her and his attentions pleased her. He did not ask for her confidence but she felt he understood and he looked at her tenderly and compassionately. She liked his reserved and respectful attitude towards her, such a contrast to the free and easy manners around her.

Since the Wan Hei Lo picnic, he was the only person with whom she exchanged ought but the barest commonplaces. He had not sought her confidence but she had shown him a corner of her bruised heart and he had found simple words that acted as a balm on her wounds.

He was the first to break the silence, asking her to admire the Heavens studded with thousands of stars shedding a dim light from the sky. He named the stars to her, the Greater Bear, Orion, the Swan. Then he spoke of his travels, his last visit to the Dutch Indies where he had stayed some time. In six months his contract with the Chinese Government would expire and he would return to Holland and take up his duties again as engineer in the Dykes Administration.

Meanwhile, Borioni talked to de Wolf, whose wife, staid and chilly, listened without flinching to the most awful stories being told her by Graziolli. Encouraged by her attitude the young Italian had slyly taken advantage of the darkness to promenade an indiscreet hand over certain rotundities, which did not appear to shun this attention. As however, he became bolder in his actions, she said simply without raising her voice:

"Please bring me a glass of lemonade, there is some on the tray over there."

Mme. de Beaurelois wanted some too and as he handed her a glass she asked:

"You have just spent a week in Pei Ta Ho. What is it like this year?"

He needed no pressing and answered immediately:

"It is quite lively, nearly all the British Legation is there. But I did not see much of them. You know, they live all together, somewhat isolated, at the beach. I went to play tennis with them once or twice. But the beautiful Mrs. Brixton is a great success; she is in splendid form and only thinks of arranging parties and picnics."

"Oh, who is there now?

"Maugrais, of course," and he smiled to show he was aware of all the intrigues.

"Oh, I forgot to tell you there is much talk about their leaving! Brixton has been appointed somewhere else and they go home via America. Young Maxwell is delighted. He is recalled to Washington and intends to travel with them. By the way, I think he is after her. If I were Maugrais, I should begin to worry. I also saw Chatours. I thought he was tamed, but I find him quite queer again now. He walks on the beach, talking to himself and gesticulating. I joined him one evening to smoke cigar in his company. He told me China was a deceptive country; he had exhausted all its charm, and meant to gather new impressions under different climes. He spoke of travelling, of his nostalgia for the ocean and other nonsense. Do you know, I fancy he must be a little cracked."

He rambled on, without any idea of the pain he was inflicting on two hearts. Mrs. Immersteht interrupted him to ask what had become of the de Maricourts.

"They are in Japan," answered Mme. de Beaurelois, glad of an excuse to change the conversation. I received a postcard from them this morning, it bore the Miyajima post mark, you know the Sacred Island of the Inland Sea where tame deer walk about everywhere, even in the village streets. They are delighted with the country and intend to make the grand tour, Kyoto, Nikko and return by way of Kobe and Shanghai."

Turning to Dr. Borioni, she asked him what he had been doing all day. No one had seen him, he had not been to the Temple with the others. The old man took his inseparable pipe from his lips for a second and answered jokingly: "Good gracious, dear lady, I can keep nothing from you. This is how my day was spent. After lunch I stayed here and took a nap; at four o'clock I bathed; when I came out of the water, I went on the Great Wall and lying down in the wild grasses I mused as I read some Chinese classics."

"Please," said Mme. Immersteht, who for nothing on earth would have missed an opportunity to improve her mind, "tell us the history of the Great Wall." The doctor required a little urging for he hated making a display of his knowledge. But as she insisted he rapped his pipe sharply against the stone table to empty it and began:

"Cheng, coming to the throne in 246 B.C. undertook this great work. Having conquered and annexed all the tributary states, he founded a vast Empire on the ruins of the feudal system prevailing until then. The former dynasty having fire as their emblem, he chose water as his, because water extinguishes fire and as the number six corresponds with the water symbol, all combinations were obliged to have that number as a basis. At the time, the Tartars, Hsung Hou, who later ravaged Europe under the name of the Huns, were making raids on the frontiers. They were a nomad race and, thoroughly warlike, were a menace to the new Empire."

"Cheng becoming Emperor Shi Hwang Ti, made up his mind to raise an impassable barrier before them. At his call, more than a million men started work and in a comparatively few years they built this Great Wall which begins at the sea and finishes in the Kansu, a distance of nearly 1400 kilometres. The story goes that the Emperor first consulted an oracle before deciding to raise this formidable rampart. The oracle told him that his dynasty would be over-thrown by the Huns, but, as in the time of the ancient Greeks, the gods expressed themselves in ambiguous terms. The character used to designate the Huns could also be employed for the name of the Emperor's second son. For a long time the Northern hordes dashed themselves against the Great Wall as the waves against the cliff however, the work of the haughty sovereign who had decreed his family should remain in power until the ten thousandth generation, was destroyed but two years after the death of the creator of the New Empire. The oracle spoke truly; the younger son of Shih Hwang Ti assassinated his elder brother and seized the throne. He was killed by a eunuch from the Palace and the new Han dynasty took the place of the one that in the mind of its founder should have reigned over China for centuries."

SILHOUETTES OF PEKING

Pausing a moment to think, the old man added: Here, at Shan Hai Kwan, 'The Mountain Toll,' 1800 years later, that is 1644 of our era, the fate of the Ming dynasty was decided. A rebellion, started in the Western Provinces spread; the chief rebel, General Li, reached the walls of Peking; a traitor opened the gates and the city became the prey of flames. From the top of the Coal Hill the Emperor was anxiously watching, hoping to catch a glimpse of the troops recalled from the North; he looked upon the scene of murder and carnage. Knowing his fate, he returned mournful but quite resigned, to his Palace. He made up his mind that neither he nor his family should fall alive into the hands of the rebels. Calling the Empress he handed her the fatal string and ordered the strangling of his chief concubines; he had the strange courage to kill his daughter with his own hands."

"He passed the night in prayer; the first thing next morning, he ascended the Coal Hill once more. The sound of the rams beating against the Palace gates could easily be heard. Without flinching, he sent for his writing materials and with a firm hand, he wrote in his own blood a few words asking his happy rival to do what he pleased with his Imperial body, but to spare his people. Then untying his silken sash, he hanged himself on a cypress tree nearby; it can still be seen with a chain placed on it by the Manchu Emperors as a reminder of the sacrilegious murder to which the tree was an accessory."

"But the rebel chief wished to destroy completely the last defenders of the Empire, who arriving too late to save the Capital had fled to the North. At the head of 100,000 men he followed them and came up to them at Shan Hai

Kwan. The head of the Imperial troops had sought refuge here and was negociating with the Manchus for their aid. Their Prince would not commit himself and would promise nothing; the battle began without his abandoning his neutrality. More than 400,000 men met; for a long time the struggle was undecided; towards noon both sides were equal."

"At this moment from the heights whence he viewed the battle, the Manchu Prince made a sign to his formidable cavalry. They hurled themselves into the fray on the side of the Imperial troops. In a few minutes they had swept the battle field. The rebels were forced back to Peking where the Manchus soon followed and a month after the battle of Shan Hai Kwan, General Li and his troops fled to Shansi; the rebellion was quelled. An impressive funeral was given the last Ming Emperor, but the Throne was empty. A Manchu Prince was called to fill it and founded the Tsing dynasty, made famous later by Kang Hsi and Chien Lung."

Borioni ceased speaking; he began to fill his everlasting little pipe once more.

Every one was delighted with the story and Mme. Immersteht felt obliged to compliment him.

"What a wonderful memory you have, my dear Doctor," she said, "you are a perfect well of science. You have unveiled for us just now all the 'arcanes' of the history of China." She said *arcades* instead of *arcanes*. She would scatter learned words in her conversation and usually make terrible blunders, to the great joy of her hearers. She went on: "Do you think the people were happier in the time of Kang Hsi or Chien Lung than to-day?" The old man, buried in his thoughts, avoided the question.

De Wolf took upon himself to answer. Dried up, but still alert though over sixty, he had lived nearly 20 years in Peking, without having succeeded in doing any business, but he was still enthusiastic over China's developement. Always looking for new mining or railway concessions, his pockets were stuffed with contracts that never came to anything. His wife had only joined him a few years ago; she had stayed in Europe, said de Wolf, to look after the children's education. Their friends said that her prolonged stay over there had something to do with the constancy of an old admirer who was interested in more ways than one in the husband's syndicates.

"Dear lady, there is no question about it. Thanks to the foreigners, China is getting accustomed to our ideas of civilization; she is advancing very fast! Merchants and bankers have been followed by engineers; railways already run through part of the country; quite lately thousands of miles of railroad have been conceded and the time is not far off when a ribbon of iron will unite Peking and Canton and open up communications between Chinese Turkestan and the Maritime Provinces." He waved his arms about as if he was tracing the railway lines on an imaginary map.

"The people are not indifferent to these signs of progress, for they foresee the consequences. They understand that from now the mining resources of the country can be exploited and they know their value. I have just been in the Honan; there are mines of untold richness there; I made a survey for the group I represent."

He continued speaking, no one paid any attention. Immersteht interrupted him with a grim joke. "All your contracts," he said, "will never be worth as much as a perpetual grant in a cemetery and while awaiting the eternal slumber, I am going to ask these ladies for permission to retire to bed."

They were all tired so they followed his example. Mme. de Beaurelois stayed alone with Miss de Frissonges and Axel. The Dutchman asked the girl shyly, "Are you going to bed at once?"

Miss de Frissonges replied "No, it is nice and cool, I shall remain here a little longer with Mme. de Beaurelois if she will allow me." He wanted to stay with them, but afraid of being in the way, he said good night and vanished behind the boy who took him to the end courtyard where the bachelors had their sleeping quarters.

Blanche had scarcely joined in the conversation at all that evening. She had been languid and mournful, lost in thought. Now every one had departed, she felt an urgent need to talk, to be consoled like a child wanting to be petted to help it forget its troubles. She knew the girl was suffering from Maugrais' neglect, as she was from Chatours' deceit. With unconscious selfishness she wanted to be pitied by some one whose heart was bleeding too. But her maternal instinct and also a sort of modesty held her back, she was rather ashamed; some one else's wounds needed healing. She took the girl's hand, it was hanging down beside the arm of the wicker chair; pressing it, she said: "Well, my poor dear, you seem quite distressed, I know you are in trouble; you have altered so much this summer. You used to be so cheery and now you have become serious and almost dull. Come, pull yourself together. At your age such behaviour cannot be allowed."

Miss de Frissonges did not reply, but Mme. de Beaurelois could see an expression of pain flit through her eyes. She grew affectionate. "Look here, little girl, between women, there can never be any secrets. You lost your little fair head over a nice young man, who, after seeming to share the feelings he had awakened, stupidly let himself become entangled with an old woman. Well, is that such a terrible misfortune? You are not yet twenty. If that man could not appreciate you, it was because he was unworthy of you. At your age nothing is lost and you will easily find some one who will understand you and will not hesitate to marry you."

"Oh, yes, of course, you are right, and I told myself the same thing the day after I discovered the American had taken him from me; but I cannot help it, it is stronger than I am. You see, I did not quite realize the nature of my feelings for him, but I was so happy to be with him and to talk to him. At the same time some instinct made me hate that woman who always seemed to come between us. As soon as I was certain he had given me up, I knew I loved him. Oh, it was awful, I felt as if the ground had given way beneath my feet and I was falling into space. For days I went about mechanically, doing the everyday things of life, but at nights when I went to bed and when I found myself at last alone with my thoughts, I would sob and sob and often the first rays of the morning sun would find me still in tears. After such nights my father would increase my anguish by asking me a thousand questions because I did not look well." She paused for a moment, then she continued: "If only he had realized how I could have loved him. I would have been his devoted companion and I would have tried to raise myself to his level."

As she said these last words, her hoarse voice broke as if the vision of the happiness she had missed stopped the words in her throat.

"Poor little thing," said Blanche very moved, "Time will help you to forget." Then feeling the need of consolation too, she went on: "You are not the only person here who is in trouble. Others are victims also of the inconstancy and ingratitude of men. As you grow older, you will see how little they deserve the affection we lavish on them. Alas, we women are often led astray by our impulses." She paused and then as if to herself she added: "I too have been deceived by an ungrateful man and now I am alone, without any one to care for me."

"But you are young and beautiful," said Miss de Frissonges. "Every one here admires you and you will always be surrounded by adorers." Then continuing unconsciously Mme. de Boaurelois' own arguments, she said: "Time heals many wounds, you will find some other affection to replace the one you have lost!" Blanche sighed, then as if suddenly inspired. "You know, little one, what you need is not a Jean Maugrais. You need a nice young man like the Dutchman who adores you. Don't deny it, I have watched him lately. Under a cold exterior he hides a heart of gold; he would make you very happy."

"Yes, may be, but I am still too sore to think of anything but my troubles. Please don't talk about that sort of thing, it is not kind. My wounds have not yet healed, I don't want to think of anything else just now."

Neither spoke; they yielded to the influence of the calm and still night; their nerves relaxed. A kind of numbness, the kind a sick person experiences after a crisis, crept gradually over them. The peace of the darkness took possession of them, veiling their painful memories which were already becoming blurred.

Over the Great Wall, above the Manchurian Hills, the moon, wending its way, suddenly appeared out of the clouds. A soft and gentle light fell over the terrace covering the whole and awakening all sleeping nature.

Both the women had the same feeling; with the pale moon rays, forerunner of more brilliant light, a glimmer of hope entered their hearts, expectant of a triumphant dawn.

But though the girl, her eyes half closed, regretfully allowed herself to be encouraged by consoling thoughts, Blanche, on the contrary, had already forgotten the past and, conscious of her rôle of "Grande Amoureuse" she began to think of her future conquests.

Proving the justice of La Bruyère's thought — of which she had probably never heard — "A woman forgets all of a man she no longer loves, even to the favours she has bestowed upon him," she felt quite indifferent to Chatours now and, her thoughts busy about her future choice, she tried visualize his features.

SILHOUETTES OF PEKING

CHAPTER X

MAUGRAIS walked slowly down Legation Street on the shady side, for it was three o'clock and this beautiful autumn afternoon was still hot. The wind from Mongolia had blown for two days, covering all the city in a yellow fog which the feeble rays of an almost blue sun could hardly pierce. When this desert wind descends on the city, the whole of Peking, swept by violent blasts, is smothered in a dusty symphony of blue and yellow.

Maugrais had passed these two days stretched on his sofa, a closed book on his knee, listening to the roaring wind and the noise of the rolled up matting of the *pang* as it rattled against the bamboo poles like the rustling of the wings of an affrighted bird. He had only been last night to the Chien Men station to bid farewell to the Brixtons. Now that the wind had fallen and Peking had resumed its normal aspect, he had gone out to breathe this reviving pure autumnal air one drinks in like a glass of champagne and which puts into the blood a longing for happiness and a desire to live.

Reaching the Jade Canal, he turned down under the trees to the left opposite the British Legation; the street was empty, it was cool under the acacias. He leant on the parapet and his eyes wandered over the green and muddy water. Then the entire scene of the Brixton's departure came to his mind. The station was crowded, all Peking had come in spite of the bad weather. The President had sent his orchestra; the musicians in their scarlet clothes, blocking the platform with their instruments, waited for a signal from their conductor. The guard of honour, composed of tall, scraggy Sikhs, was drawn up and a crowd pressed round the special car attached to the back of the train in which the British Councillor was to travel. The whole official world, both Chinese and European was there. Many friends and still more onlookers. He saw Mrs. Brixton in a grey travelling dress standing on the platform of the station, a large blue veil over her hat. She conversed with some of the wives of the diplomats; her arms were full of flowers. Her husband in light brown and a felt hat, both hands in his pockets, his eternal cigar between his lips listened to the last phrases of the three foreign Office Officials who were there.

Maugrais pushed his way through the crowd, shaking hands as he went, and climbed into the train in the hopes of catching Mrs. Brixton alone if only for a few seconds. He entered the narrow corridor full of suit cases and flowers, searching for the American. He found her maid, a hat box in her hand; she looked worried.

"Is this Mrs. Brixton's compartment?" he asked.

She nodded and he went in. She seemed to understand what he meant to do, for she put the box on the bed and disappeared. Maugrais sat down and waited, a murmur of voices came from outside. He could hear laughter, promises being exchanged, expressions of regret. Lost in thought, regardless of everything around him, he closed his eyes. He opened them again and saw the hat box with two labels on the bed, Nikko - Kanaya Hotel - Shanghai, Astor House.

"And now it is finished," he said aloud.

"What is finished?" asked Mrs. Brixton, standing before him. Slender, energetic, sweet and obstinate, she looked at him, crumpled up on the sofa. She sat down beside him and suddenly held out both her hands. In this gesture, there was a mixture of comradeship and some sporting element. Then Maugrais tried to remember all he meant to say in this supreme moment, all he had cherished in his heart during long days of solitude. But all his ideas had flown, he felt only a great emptiness seized him. However he made an effort to speak. "Lucy, Lucy," he said, "I must speak to you."

She interrupted him and holding his hands tightly in both of her:

"Jean, I want to ask something of you. . ."

There was an earnest prayer in her eyes.

"I want you not to say a word. . . but to take that suit case out of the rack because otherwise it will fall on my head as soon as the train moves."

Mechanically Maugrais obeyed. As he got off the seat, the husband appeared in the doorway.

"Lucy, the train is about to start," he said without seeming to notice the young man. "I am coming," she answered and followed Brixton, leaving Jean where he was, the suit case in his hands. A moment later, the shrill whistle blew, the train began to move, the band struck up, handkerchiefs waved and a surging mass of people went down the station after the carriage on the platform of which Mrs. Brixton stood smiling. Her modest and generous smile spoke of triumph, of forgetfulness and pardon.

And now leaning on the bridge over the Jade Canal Maugrais recalled all the details of Mrs. Brixton's departure, a great bitterness entered his soul. He closed his eyes, seized with a violent desire to feel no more, to live no longer. A few minutes afterwards, he crossed the wooden bridge opposite the British Legation and went off in the direction of Legation Street.

"What changes there have been these last few weeks," he said to himself. "The Brixtons have gone, the Wolfs are on their way to South America, the Beaurelois are on leave, the de Frissonges have left with the Dutchman, Axel; so much in love with the girl."

He recalled the tender and melancholy outline of Melle de Frissonges; he could see her fragile body possessed of such a strong soul, loving and shy; he could see her with her great blue eyes, trying to understand life so as to be able to love it and to believe in it. He had a wild hallucination of a happy home in the Alps opposite an immense blue sea.

He saw all his friends had gone and he received the impression that life had taken a step forward, leaving him behind, abandoned and useless. He walked quicker, his heart wrung with anguish. He wanted to meet some one he knew, to shake a friendly hand, to be no longer alone with his grim thoughts and his vivid regrets. As he neared Legation Street, he saw a man rush out of the Wagons Lits Hotel, pause on the steps and make mad signs to him with a piece of paper or a card which he flourished in the air, at same time he whirled his stick above his head. Jean recognized Chatours.

"Oh, yes, he has not left us yet. Suppose I go and see him." That was his first thought.

"Jean, Jean," called Chatours, "come here at once; look at this and congratulate me."

His somewhat eccentric face, his whole changeable expression shone with glee. "But whatever is the matter," asked Jean, trying to see what it was that Chatours still waved wildly over his head. "Did you win the Chinese Internal Loan Lottery?"

"Not a bit of it," cried Chatours I booked my passage, "as the English tourists say. Look at this pocket book, it represents 120 days of travel across two oceans, calling at ports in the green islands of Polynesia, halts in the Brazilian harbours burning with passion and fever, passing though the Straits of Magellan between enormous rocks covered with ice; and finally the immense expanse of new horizons, skies studded with new constellations, vast mines of unknown sensations. It means space, it means freedom."

He shouted all this, standing on the steps of the hotel, frantically brandishing his cane. Tourists, coming out to get into the motors waiting to take them to the Summer Palace, stopped, uneasy but happy to think they were witnessing some scandalous scene. Maugrais paused, thunderstruck. He knew of course that Chatours was leaving; he knew he had broken with the Baroness and that he was tired of Marchioness Ting, but somehow he expected Chatours would be sorry to go and that before his departure he would pass long hours dreaming on the Wall over the Imperial City, make pilgrimages to favourite temples, where, in the shadows, Bodisatwas stretched forth their arms towards the vast Heavens and Kuan Yin looked down upon mournful humanity from between their drooping eyelids. He pictured him going to the beloved tombs where, buried in deep vaults below magnificent yellow roofed ruins, sleep forever in peace the remains of Imperial tyrants whose short life had been an oriental medley of murder and lust. He expected a heart-rending leave-taking, poignant farewells . . . instead he saw before him a Chatours bubbling over with joy!

It was the black ingratitude of the passing soul who has already escaped to other climes, leaving behind it only its earthly wrapping to go through the formalities of a hasty departure. He could see those eyes which not so long ago reflected the traditional poses of Buddha seated in the shadow of the temple, the tottering old palaces in ruins by the sacred lakes, those lakes full of lotus under whose large leaves the mortal remains of some abandoned Princess or some jealous eunuch rested in the mud. Those eyes had reflected the sombre and sad line of the wall along which the caravans of camels wending their way through the golden lanes, finished their dreams in the arid sand of the Gobi desert. Those eyes seemed to burn now with a new flame, kindled by the phosphorescent light of a tropical sea.

Maugrais, finding nothing to say, mutely held out his hand. But Chatours, without noticing the gesture, had already jumped into a rickshaw and, kicking the coolie to make him hurry, turned round for the last time, his pocket book in his hand and shouted his favourite verses from Mallarme: "Fuir là-bas, fuir, je sens que les oiseaux sont ivres d'être parmi l'écume inconnue et les cieux . . . ."

The remainder was interrupted by the hooting of a horn. A large motor car pulled up before the hotel; still humming, it discharged a noisy crowd of American tourists. Chatours had vanished. Maugrais cast a miserable glance about him, a glance that seemed to try and catch a friendly eye, then he slowly went back towards the Chinese city.

He soon reached the narrow hutungs of the Western city, walking in a dream and pausing mechanically from time to time before the fruit-seller's stall and the shop windows of a curio dealer, keeping to one side to allow some slow and stately camels to pass. He was surprised to find himself suddenly in front of Count de Cordobas' door. He hesitated, should he knock? Then he struck the metal plate. The old *kai men ti* came to open, without undue haste, a kind fatherly smile on his lips. A crowd of children followed him; they greeted Maugrais with shrill cries of joy. He remembered giving a dollar to those children, more than a year ago. He crossed the two small paved courtyards and found himself before the peaceful and shady pavilion at the end. He opened the door. Crossing the first room which was in solemn semi-darkness, he knocked on the door of the next room where five months ago Mrs. Brixton had smoked opium! A well known voice bade him enter. Cordobas clad in a dark silk kimono and a black haori, was standing in front of a cage containing a magnificent multi-coloured parrot; he had bought it years ago outside Shun Chih Men. The bird climbed up the bars of its cage with the help of its hooked beak; every now and again he gave shrill guttural cries. His master seemed to understand them. He smiled at Jean and pointing to the bird: "As talkative as a woman but so much more intelligent, more faithful, and above all, more independent in its opinions."

"Do you understand what it is saying," asked Jean, ensconcing himself among the many cushions of the Turkish divan.

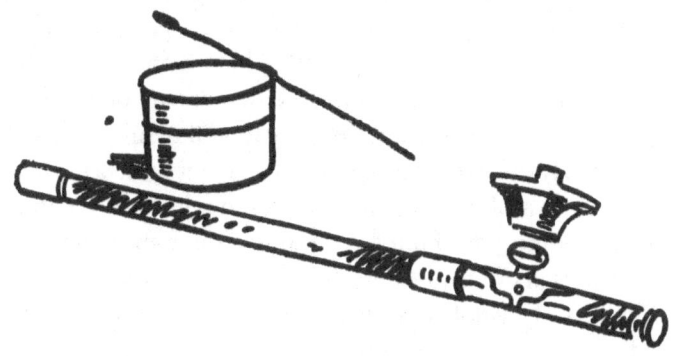

"Of course," replied the Count I have just donned this kimono and he is thanking me because he knows it means I am staying at home. But when I put on my evening clothes he utters piercing screams and beats his wings against the bars of his cage because he knows I shall be absent for some hours."

The Count scratched the bird's neck, ruffling its feathers with his nail.

"He has loved this ring for years," he went on, showing a magnificent emerald he wore on his fourth finger. "When he is annoyed or nervous, I need only pass the ring between the bars of his cage, and he calms down at once and his blue green eyes, so false yet so soft, gaze at the stone and he murmurs gently to it. The soul of the beast is closer to the soul of a mineral than ours. It is possible there is some silent communion between them."

He lighted a cigarette and took a chair opposite the great Buddha. A long silence ensued and then Maugrais said as if to himself. It was here, lying on this sofa that she smoked opium so madly; her lips closed, her eyes fixed on the ceiling, she was planning her revenge and I know now that her heart was in a whirl of hatred and passion, of desire and despair. Only a few months have gone by, but good Heavens, how short yet how long the time seems. A whole lifetime is contained in those five months, a whole long life. And I have neither the desire nor the strength to begin another. But I am forced to live on, I am obliged to drag myself from place to place, to talk, to think, to eat, when I only want to sleep, to sleep the sleep of Nature. What is there in life to interest me? To whom can I attach myself? To what can I aspire, what can I desire when all around me is bleak and dreary?"

From the depths of his armchair, Cordobas answered gravely: "Often when we are nearest salvation we feel more hopeless; often when the soul is already in a state of grace it throws itself desperately back into the shadows, dazzled by the radiant light flooding it. My child, the mystics of the Middle Ages knew of this state and in their tender forcible language they called it 'the soul's dark night.'

Once past that crisis the neophyte has a glimpse of mystic joys, those unforgettable joys that can only be attained after the renunciation of all desires and the suppression of all passion. The Masters of the Indies also experienced this dark depression, it precedes the entry of the new disciple into the third of the seven portals — the Kshanti — on the road leading to unutterable bliss, perfect peace, the Samyak Samboddhi."

As he pronounced these words he rose. Coming towards the sad faced Buddha he said "Perfect peace, incomparable bliss. Anuttera Samyak Samboddhi." Turning to Maugrais, he murmured, "Purify your heart and spirit. When you have made *tabula rasa* of your soul and driven out from your heart every vain desire, you will stand upon the first rung of the ladder that leads man to Heaven. Quite empty must be your brain and the Great Understanding will make its home there. You will become as a volcano in the moon, then love will flood you with a burning tide. When you shall no longer have within your brain a thought, no longer a spark of passion in your flesh then and then alone, will Peace, the Queen of the Universe, set up her Throne within your heart." He walked straight up to Maugrais, pale, dark, almost threatening. "When you desire no more riches, honours, love, nor men's esteem, when you long no more for happiness, when your ears have become deaf even to the prayers of men, then you will hear the voice of Brahma. When your eyes become blind to the beauty of nature, to the deeds of mankind, when they no longer shed a tear, then you will behold the Eternal. When your heart has ceased to beat and such dark shadows drown your soul that it desires not even Nirvana — that age-long, blissful trance — then, my son, you will have entered the path of Truth that leads to Eternal Peace."

He stood before Maugrais, an hour passed, neither spoke. Then Jean lifted his head, up to now buried in the cushions and murmured softly, "Cordobas, Cordobas." The Count, lost in thought, did not reply. "Cordobas, like a frightened child fallen at your feet, I cry to you, Cordobas, is there a God?" A long, mournful silence ensued. The

autumn afternoon was drawing to a close and twilight was creeping over the room. The great Buddha, seated on his lotus flower, pointed with his uplifted arm to the far off, mute, inexorable sky.

Jean rose, he tried to distinguish Cordoba's features.

"Cordobas, you have not answered me. I knocked and you did not open."

He fell back again on to the sofa, his head in the cushions. Then the voice of the Count, gentler and more solemn, sounded in his ears: "One day Milinda, all powerful King of the Indies tortured by doubt, worn out by passion, visited Ananda, who lived in the Himalayas. Forgetting his royal state, the laws and customs of his country, he threw himself at Ananda's feet and cried: 'Ananda, the entire Indies acclaims you as their Spiritual Head. You are alive in the three worlds and you have crossed the Threshold more than 10,000 years ago. Prompted by a desire to help suffering mankind, you chose to return to this world of misery when you might be sleeping peacefully in the Great Resting Place of the World, the Nirvana of the Sages. Mahatma, you have attained perfect knowledge. See, I am at your feet devoured by passion, tortured by doubt, consumed by desire, and you, by a word, can give back peace to my mind and tranquility to my soul. The King of the Indies is your slave, but answer his question, Ananda, is there a God Creator of the World and Men, an all powerful, merciful God?' "

"He ceased speaking. Ananda did not reply. The King put the question a second, then a third time, but Ananda did not heed. The King, mournful and angry, rose: 'Ananda, did you not hear? Why refuse to speak?

Is it perhaps because you cannot answer?' Then the Sage spoke: 'King Milinda, I have heard your question, I have replied, but you did not understand.' He turned his back to the King and disappeared into his cave cut in the rock."

Maugrais rose and stared open-eyed at the Count. A few minutes went by, then staggering like a drunken man he left the room, crossing the hall, the two small courtyards and found himself in the street.

He walked along the Hutungs, his head low, staring at the paving stones; his brain was numb, his heart empty. He felt as if the great void mentioned by Cordobas had begun to invade him. He reached the Wall, climbed it and went towards the West.

There was no one about, the grass had been cut and he could see as far as the tower which forms the South West angle of the city. He was glad to be alone. He stopped, raised his head and took deep breaths, inhaling the fresh evening air. Then he went slowly on, leaving behind him the Legation Quarter. Night was approaching, dark and dignified night. He paused and looked about him. A deep peace seemed to descend from the blue sky with the twilight and spread over the Peking plain, that country of a beauty so unassuming, so gay yet so sad, that plain where sleep, in their tombs, the humble generations that are no more. The sun was sinking gloriously into its couch of purple and gold, behind the hills now all blue. On the other side of the Wall, Peking was stirring, Peking so gentle at evening when the half ruined houses and the old trees bending over the walls become shrouded in shadows as if falling into oblivion. The mysterious tragic cry of Peking, that cry of a thousand sounds, calls of merchants, squeaking of carts, tam-tam of temple gongs, braying of donkeys, singing of beggars that cry of Peking, that is life and music, rose from the still animated streets below.

Maugrais seated himself on the edge of the Wall, his eyes closed. He seemed to absorb all that life of Peking, he could hear buzzing so near, yet so distant.

An hour passed, he did not move; his whole person seemed glued to the spot, then his eyes opened and he

murmured Cordobas' words: "Peace, everlasting peace." He closed his eyes again and any one seeing him thus, his legs crossed, his hands folded, his gaze vacant, would have taken him for a Fakir come from some Indian Temple to meditate silently on this wall above the Imperial Palace, that city of a past splendour, that city of dreams, of death, of passion.

Lost in contemplation Maugrais sat motionless on the Wall. A flight of pigeons rose over Peking and came towards him. On the white birds small pipes, fluting through the air, gave out thin harp like notes. It was as music from Heaven. And this gentle flock scattered over Maugrais' head like petals from a great white lotus; then forming a line, the birds circled in graceful curves round him like a silver halo. They came lower and lower, brushing against him with their wings mistaking him belike, so still he sat, for one of those marble statues that guard the ancient tombs of Kings or for some image of a Buddha seated, mute and solitary, meditating upon the sufferings of men.

Shedding a benediction from their snowy wings, the doves soared slowly into the air and homed back to Peking already shrouded in the dusk, and behind them, filling the limpid evening air trilled the bell-like music of their flight.

www.ingramcontent.com/pod-product-compliance
Lightning Source LLC
LaVergne TN
LVHW030321070526
838199LV00069B/6519